# THEODORE
# ROOSEVELT,
# CEO

# THEODORE ROOSEVELT, CEO

## 7 PRINCIPLES TO GUIDE AND INSPIRE MODERN LEADERS

### ALAN AXELROD

STERLING
New York

STERLING
New York

An Imprint of Sterling Publishing
387 Park Avenue South

ISBN 978-1-4027-8483-5 (hardcover)
ISBN 978-1-4027-9100-0 (ebook)

**Library of Congress Cataloging-in-Publication Data**

Axelrod, Alan, 1952-
  Theodore Roosevelt, CEO : 7 principles to guide and inspire modern leaders / Alan
Axelrod.
    p. cm.
  Includes index.
  ISBN 978-1-4027-8483-5
  1. Leadership. 2. Chief executive officers. 3. Roosevelt, Theodore, 1858-1919. I. Title.
HD57.7.A965 2012
658.4'092--dc23

                    2011033142

Distributed in Canada by Sterling Publishing
c/o Canadian Manda Group, 165 Dufferin Street
Toronto, Ontario, Canada M6K 3H6
Distributed in the United Kingdom by GMC Distribution Services
Castle Place, 166 High Street, Lewes, East Sussex, England BN7 1XU
Distributed in Australia by Capricorn Link (Australia) Pty. Ltd.
P.O. Box 704, Windsor, NSW 2756, Australia

For information about custom editions, special sales, and premium
and corporate purchases, please contact Sterling Special Sales at 800-805-5489 or
specialsales@sterlingpublishing.com.

Manufactured in the United States of America

2  4  6  8  10  9  7  5  3  1

Courtesy Library of Congress, Prints & Photographs Division: FRONTISPIECE: President
Theodore Roosevelt speaking from his car at Lake City, Minnesota, 1903 (LC-DIG-
stereo-1s02081); DEDICATION PAGE: Roosevelt at his desk in the White House, c. 1902
(LC-DIG-stereo-1s01917). CHAPTER OPENERS: Engraving by Sidney L. Smith, c. 1905
(LC-DIG-pga-03324)

*For Anita and Ian*

# CONTENTS

# Introduction
## *The Emphatic Executive*

"While President I have been President, emphatically; I have used every ounce of power there was in the office."

~ Theodore Roosevelt

He was born in the family brownstone at 28 East 20th Street, Manhattan, on October 27, 1858. From the beginning, his survival was in question. Childhood asthma, both frequent and severe, continually threatened to strangle him, so that he was unable to sleep flat in a bed, but had to prop himself on a mountain of pillows. Chronic congenital diarrhea—the family termed it, more genteelly, "cholera morbus"—contributed to his ghostly complexion and undersized physique. That frail frame was often assailed by high fevers and racking coughs.

Physicians were doubtful that Theodore Roosevelt would reach his fourth year. But the child endured. He endured patiently at first; then, as he approached his teen years, fiercely.

When he was about twelve, his father took him aside. "Theodore, you have the mind"—for his son was an avid reader and a remarkably quick study—"but you have not the body, and without the help of the body the mind cannot go as far as it should. You

[1]

must make your body. It is hard drudgery to make one's body," father cautioned son, "but I know you will do it."

Theodore promised his father and himself that he would "do it," and, without hesitation, embarked on a program of exercise. Relentless walking, running, weight lifting, and calisthenics seemed destined either to build him up or lay him low. The boy worked himself daily to the very verge of collapse. As an adult, he would call this approach to living "the strenuous life," and he enthusiastically recommended it to anyone who intended to make something of himself. The idea was starkly simple: use every ounce of power you had every time you did anything. If the unremitting effort threatened to kill you, so much the better. As Roosevelt would write to his friend Cecil Spring-Rice years later, "Death is always and under all circumstances a tragedy, for if it is not, then it means that life itself has become one." There could be no genuine reward without real risk.

The popular mythology that has grown up around Teddy Roosevelt holds that, through dint of sheer physical and mental will, he utterly transformed himself from a sickly child into a strapping young man. The myth comes surprisingly close to reality—not that the transformation was rapid or easy, however. Even as he built himself up, relapses into asthma and "cholera morbus" were frequent. During a European trip with his family, Teedie (as his mother and siblings affectionately called him) started wheezing so badly that Mrs. Roosevelt confided desperately to Anna Minkowitz, who served as governess and tutor during the family's overseas sojourn, "I wonder what will become of my Teedie." The young woman calmly replied, "You need not be anxious about him. He will surely one day be a great professor, or who knows, he may become even President of the United States."

It was the first such prediction recorded, but certainly not the last. Even in illness, when to all appearances, the prospects for survival into adulthood were in gravest doubt, there was an air of destiny about the boy. Moreover, it clearly seemed a destiny that

[2]

would be of his own making. If he could will himself to survive, he could will himself to become strong, and if he could do that, he could certainly will himself to be whatever he chose to be, including the American president.

◼

Teedie stormed through Harvard College from 1876 to 1880, earning renown as a collegiate boxer and graduating magna cum laude, finding time as well to write his first book, *The Summer Birds of the Adirondacks in Franklin County, N.Y.*, which was published in his sophomore year. Before he graduated, he began a second book on a very different subject, *The Naval War of 1812*. He studied hard. He boxed hard. The death of his father from stomach cancer on February 9, 1878, was a tough blow, but it only encouraged him to push himself harder.

Shortly after graduating, he married the beautiful Alice Hathaway Lee and then entered Columbia Law School (though he left after two years without taking his degree). He had, by this time, already thrown himself into Republican politics and, in 1881, was elected to the New York State Assembly, the youngest assemblyman in the state's history.

He set out to make himself conspicuous in Albany, at first by the showy opulence of his attire, suited more to grand opera than to the legislature. A "New York City dude," his legislative colleagues called him, and they snickered, even as their attention was drawn, focused, and utterly monopolized by him. From day one, freshman Roosevelt spoke up in the assembly. Within days of that first day, he was proposing legislation and was soon writing one bill after another, while also finding the time to complete and publish his book, *The Naval War of 1812*. That volume was instantly snapped up by the U.S. Naval Academy and assigned to midshipmen as a required textbook.

Reelected to the assembly by a margin wider than that of any other legislator in 1883, he was named minority leader, and, after touring the slums of New York City with union organizer Samuel Gompers, composed and championed a series of groundbreaking public welfare bills. Then, when the assembly recessed, he went out West—way out west, to the Dakota Territory Badlands, bought two ranches there, and worked them alongside the other cowboys, taking time off to hunt bison on the prairie.

In the assembly, he had made powerful enemies among the machine politicians of both parties who were desperate to bolster the cracking walls of the status quo. In the Badlands, he faced down bison, grizzly bears, and even gunfighters. It seems he courted death—both political death and actual death—to intensify the experience of life. The harder the challenge, the more formidable the opponent, the more joyously he came on, everyone who knew him agreed, like a force of nature.

Or, rather, a force beyond nature: a veritable machine. The prominent American physician and student of Japanese culture William Sturgis Bigelow would later say that he had never known "a man with such a head of steam on," and another acquaintance marveled that Roosevelt presented the "dazzling, even appalling, spectacle of a human engine driven at full speed." That engine seized up and stopped cold on February 14, 1884. Two days earlier, his daughter, Alice Lee Roosevelt, had been born in his Manhattan home. As the cries of the newborn echoed through the house on the fourteenth, Martha Bulloch Roosevelt, Theodore's mother, died of typhoid fever. Hours later on the same day, Alice Hathaway Lee Roosevelt, his wife and now mother of his daughter, suffered kidney failure and died as well. No one had known that this vivacious young woman suffered from what was then called Bright's disease (acute nephritis), its symptoms having been masked by the usual discomforts of pregnancy.

Theodore Roosevelt, writer of books and mountains of legislation, turned to the page of his diary for February 14, 1884, drew a simple bold X in black ink and, beneath this, carefully inscribed but a single, terrible sentence: "The light has gone out of my life."

The grief would never entirely leave him, yet it also became just one more driver of renewed activity. "Black care rarely sits behind a rider whose pace is fast enough," he remarked.

■

Roosevelt proceeded with construction of a grand house in Oyster Bay, Long Island, the house in which he had intended to raise his family. "Leeholm," he was going to call it, in honor of his wife's family. With Alice gone, he decided instead to name it "Sagamore Hill" in honor of the Indian sachem who had once lived on the site.

He threw himself back into work, the human engine reigniting. The New York Republicans sent him as a delegate to the National Convention in June of 1884, and the following year he published *Hunting Trips of a Ranchman*, which would prove a bestseller, left the New York State Assembly at the end of his third term in 1885, ran for mayor of New York City the following year, and this time suffered a landslide defeat. Those close to him knew he had been badly stunned, but they also saw that, with Teddy Roosevelt, life went on. On December 2, a month after the bleak election, he married Edith Kermit Carow and, in the new year of 1887, published a new book, *Life of Thomas Hart Benton*, and saw the birth of a new child, his first son, Theodore. Uncertain of where to redirect his political ambitions, and acutely conscious of having a new mouth to feed, Roosevelt went on a well-paid writing tear, publishing three books in 1888—*Life of Gouverneur Morris*, *Ranch Life and the Hunting Trail*, and *Essays in Practical Politics*—in addition to a host of magazine articles.

He decided at length to move from state and local politics and into the national arena, accepting appointment in 1889 as U.S. civil service commissioner. It was a position he coveted because he intended singlehandedly to take on and thoroughly reform the spoils and patronage systems—long a scourge of good government— and replace them with a system of administrative appointments based solely on competence and merit. This grueling crusade would occupy the next half-dozen years—at least as his day job. He found time, in 1889, to publish the first two volumes of his monumental *The Winning of the West* (volumes three and four would appear in 1894 and 1896), which would prove the most popular of all his history books. In 1891, his *History of New York* appeared, followed in 1893 by *The Wilderness Hunter* and, two years later, *Hero Tales from American History*. A second daughter, Ethel Carow Roosevelt, was born in 1891, and a second son, Archibald Bulloch Roosevelt, in 1894, the same year that Theodore's brother, Elliott Roosevelt, an alcoholic who had always been the family black sheep, took his own life.

Work on the Civil Service Commission was at times gratifying but more often a labor of forlorn hope. On May 5, 1895, Roosevelt resigned from the commission and, the very next day, was appointed president of New York City's board of police commissioners. Here, Roosevelt felt, was a job of reform he could truly get his arms around. Although his was a municipal appointment, the New York Police Department, a veritable icon of big-city corruption, was a national scandal. A local impact here, he believed, would have nationwide effect.

The new commissioner did in New York what he could not do in Washington. He approached the problems of the police department hands on. By day, he performed administrative duties from behind his desk. By night, he personally patrolled the meanest of the city's mean streets, rousting loafing beat officers, disciplining some, praising others, and firing the unrepentant hard cases. He faced the possibility of physical assault nightly. He fended off political threats every day. Tireless and dogged, he remodeled the police department and won the support of the public. In the process, he formed close collegial relations with the remarkable cadre of progressive journalists and writers he himself would later dub the "muckrakers," including Lincoln Steffens (whose *The Shame of the Cities* exposed the corruption of urban boss government), Ida Tarbell (author of *The History of the Standard Oil Company*, a study of the predatory nature of the nation's most notorious monopolistic trust), and Jacob Riis (whose photographic and journalistic portrait of slum and sweatshop life, *How the Other Half Lives*, would have a profound effect on the role of government in promoting the public welfare).

One writer Commissioner Roosevelt encountered was neither a journalist nor a reformer—nor, for that matter, an American. He was Bram Stoker, an Irish novelist who, during an 1895 trip to the United States, came away from a meeting with Roosevelt overwhelmingly impressed. "Must be President some day," he noted. "A man you can't cajole, can't frighten, can't buy."

Two years after he met the commissioner, Bram Stoker would go on to his own enduring celebrity with the publication of *Dracula*. As for his prediction of Roosevelt's coming fame, the prospects in 1897 looked increasingly promising for its fulfillment.

■

After singlehandedly elevating the NYPD from a national disgrace to a police force that was a model for the nation's other big cities, Roosevelt resigned from the Police Board in 1897 to accept appointment by President William McKinley as assistant secretary of the navy on April 19. He approached the new assignment with the same zeal he had applied to his work as New York's top cop. He saw clearly that the United States was rapidly moving toward war with Spain over the issue of Cuban independence, and his urgent objective was to modernize the U.S. Navy through a combination of new construction and the purchase of merchant vessels that could be readily converted to warships. By law, he reported to the secretary of the navy, John Davis Long. Older and slower than his dynamic assistant, Long made the wise decision to get out of his way and gave Assistant Secretary Roosevelt the room and authority he needed to build his navy. Ordinarily, the post of assistant secretary of the navy, like that of New York City police commissioner, would have attracted little national attention. But as Roosevelt had been no ordinary police commissioner, so now he showed himself to be no ordinary assistant secretary. The public and political buzz turned increasingly presidential.

The ambitious Roosevelt, still a young man at forty, had every incentive to remain at what was proving to be a powerful, highly visible, and politically secure post—especially now that he had yet another son, Quentin, born on November 19, 1897. Yet, less than two weeks after Spain declared war on the United States on April 23, 1898, and Congress reciprocated two days later, Roosevelt, as if eager to court death yet again, resigned as assistant secretary of the navy to accept an appointment as lieutenant colonel of the 1st U.S. Volunteer Cavalry Regiment. Except for a stint with the New York National Guard, Roosevelt had no real military experience. Despite this, he plunged into the task of recruiting a force consisting mostly of cowboys from the country near his ranches, plus some former "Buffalo soldiers" (African American cavalrymen from segregated U.S. Army units), Native Americans, and, somewhat incongruously, a handful of kids from the Ivy League. He not only supervised their training, he trained alongside them, managing to keep barely a step ahead. When the regiment's CO, Colonel Leonard Wood, a career army officer, was promoted to brigade command, Roosevelt was jumped to full colonel and given command of the 1st USV, which the newspapers dubbed "The Rough Riders," a compelling nickname the new colonel and his men heartily embraced.

Colonel Roosevelt led his regiment to Cuba and to war, receiving his baptism of fire at the battle of Las Guasimas on June 24, 1898. Then came what he later called his "crowded hour." Acting on his own initiative, the colonel led his Rough Riders on a pair of charges up Kettle Hill and San Juan Hill (more properly San

Juan Heights) on July 1, an action that would be known simply as the battle of San Juan Hill. The engagement proved very bloody, but decisive. After the Rough Riders and the two other regiments of the brigade succeeded in taking the high ground, the land war in Cuba was essentially over and won.

As it happened, Colonel Roosevelt was the only member of the cavalry unit who actually had a horse to ride. It was a borrowed animal at that, as all the regular regimental mounts had been left behind on the mainland because the War Department's inept planning had resulted in a desperate shortage of transport vessels. Atop Texas (as the horse was called), Roosevelt continually exposed himself to fire. With masterful understatement, he wrote about the battle in *The Rough Riders*, published in 1899:

> A curious incident happened as I was getting the men started forward. Always when men have been lying down under cover for some time, and are required to advance, there is a little hesitation, each looking to see whether the others are going forward. As I rode down the line, calling to the troopers to go forward, and rasping brief directions to the captains and lieutenants, I came upon a man lying behind a little bush, and I ordered him to jump up. I do not think he understood that we were making a forward move, and he looked up at me for a moment with hesitation, and I again bade him rise, jeering him and saying: "Are you afraid to stand up when I am on horseback?"

> As I spoke, he suddenly fell forward on his face, a bullet having struck him and gone through him lengthwise. I suppose the bullet had been aimed at me; at any rate, I, who was on horseback in the open, was unhurt, and the man lying flat on the ground in the cover beside me was killed.

Although the shooting war stopped soon after San Juan Hill, Colonel Roosevelt found that he had to keep fighting. The same bureaucratic inefficiency that had forced the Rough Riders to enter the war without their horses now kept the regiment and many other American soldiers idly bottled up in disease-ridden Cuban jungles. As survivors of combat began to sicken and even to die of yellow fever and other jungle ailments, Roosevelt led a cadre of officers in an angry protest to Secretary of War Russell A. Alger, urging him to bring the troops home. Leaked to the press, the so-called round-robin protest letter embarrassed Alger, who did step up the evacuation effort, but who also saw to it that Roosevelt's nomination for the Medal of Honor was killed. (The decoration was finally awarded, very much posthumously, in 2001.) No matter. Thanks to extensive newspaper coverage of every aspect of the Spanish-American War, Theodore Roosevelt returned to the United States a national hero.

■

Heroically poised for major political office, Roosevelt was nominated by the Republican Party on September 27, 1898, as its candidate for New York's governor. He was elected on November 8 by a narrow margin over Democrat Augustus Van Wyck.

The nation knew, and Theodore Roosevelt knew, that the governor's mansion was a platform from which one might logically ascend to the White House. The Republican establishment knew this, too, and many of the old guard groped for a way to block the "upstart" "radical" colonel's path without alienating an adoring public's support for the party. The obvious move was to "honor" him with a high office that was nevertheless universally regarded as being of no value whatsoever. Roosevelt, accordingly, was tapped as the running mate of incumbent president William McKinley in his 1900 reelection bid.

Roosevelt was under no illusion. In an 1896 magazine article he had written that whereas the presidency was "all important," the vice presidency was "of comparatively little note" and was therefore shunned by those "most anxious" to become president. Later in life, to his friend the editor and writer Lawrence Fraser Abbott, he remarked that, having been vice president, he knew "how hollow the honor is." In 1900, he seriously considered declining the offer because he knew that it was a transparent stratagem to kill him politically by kicking him upstairs and into a dead-end office. "I would rather be in private life than Vice-President," he declared. Yet, perhaps for the very reason that it was one more opportunity to dare *political* death, he ultimately decided to accept.

The six and a half months he served as vice president were, predictably, some of the least eventful months of his political career. In September 1901, he took his family on a hiking vacation in the Adirondacks. He was on remote Mount Tahawus when word reached him on the sixth that President McKinley had been shot by a wannabe anarchist while attending the Pan-American Exposition in Buffalo, New York. Assured that the president would recover from his wounds, Roosevelt decided to continue his vacation, reasoning that to rush to McKinley's side would accomplish nothing but create a public panic.

On September 13, Vice President Roosevelt, four friends, and two park rangers were enjoying a tranquil lunch some five hundred feet above a lake named Tear-of-the-Clouds. At about 1:25, he saw another ranger running toward him, a yellow Western Union telegram clutched in his hand.

"I instinctively knew he had bad news," Roosevelt later said. "I wanted to become President, but I did not want to become President that way." The telegram announced that President William McKinley lay in "grave" condition. Late that same night, a second message would announce his death.

■

Senator Mark Hanna, kingmaker of the Republican old guard and a well-nigh worshipful friend of William McKinley, also got the news that day and that night. A year earlier, he had understood the importance of putting Roosevelt in an office from which he could do no damage to the status quo, but he had vehemently opposed positioning him a heartbeat from the White House. "Don't any of you realize," he had warned fellow party insiders in 1900, "that there's only one life between this madman and the Presidency?"

On September 14, 1901, that "one life" was gone. "Now look!" Hanna cried out, a man stricken. "That damned cowboy is president of the United States."

For his part, Theodore Roosevelt reached out to Senator Hanna, asking for his help. To the American people—and, indirectly, to the seniors of the Republican Party—he promised a continuation of the slain president's policies.

That promise turned out to be not so much a lie as, at best, a partial truth, much as Hanna's characterization of rancher Roosevelt as a "damned cowboy" had been partly true. The whole truth was that no single word could define Theodore Roosevelt or the president he would become. A man of omnivorous interests, he was certainly a "progressive" in issues social and political. McKinley had just as certainly not been. Yet, like his predecessor—and like Mark Hanna himself—Theodore Roosevelt believed whole-heartedly in capitalism, and he saw in boldly entrepreneurial enterprise as well as long-established big business the great drivers not only of the American economy but of American greatness. At the same time, and quite unlike McKinley and Hanna, he could not passively accept the party's uncritical embrace of business at the expense of labor and consumers. An embrace like that would, in the long run, smother democracy. Capitalism? By all means. But capitalism overseen by the strong stewardship of good government. Under Roosevelt, government would be active and the presidency more vigorous and thoroughly engaged than at any time since "Old Hickory," Andrew Jackson, had occupied the White House.

Thrust into the Oval Office by accidental circumstance, Roosevelt was nevertheless determined to make the very most of it.

To reverse what he saw as the descent of democracy into an oligarchy dominated by great corporate trusts and their owners, he believed it necessary to reverse what he also saw as a long decline in the power of the executive branch versus the rise of the legislative. Much as Jackson had done early in the preceding century, Roosevelt framed the role of the president as that of "steward" or "tribune." This definition was needed, he implied, because Congress no longer represented the people so much as certain special interests, namely monopolistic big business. If the members of Congress would not stand steward to the American voter, the president would and, in so doing, rescue democracy from plutocracy.

In the course of his presidency, Roosevelt fashioned what he would much later call the "New Nationalism." He expanded the role of the executive, adding to its administrative machinery for the purpose of promoting and protecting the public welfare—most notably, perhaps, when he championed passage, in 1906, of the Pure Food and Drug Act and a meat inspection law, ensuring federal protection of consumer health. To serve the people as he wanted them served, the national government would have to be conspicuously elevated above the individual states, which meant that the federal government would unambiguously trump state governments. Moreover, within the federal government, the chief executive, as people's tribune, would correct an errant Congress whenever it was caught serving special interests at the expense of the electorate.

If Roosevelt looked to Jackson as a model of a strong executive, he peered even farther back, to fellow New Yorker Alexander Hamilton, to find constitutional justification for building up the presidency as he intended to do. Hamilton had pointed out that the Constitution set *explicit* limits on the power of the presidency but was silent on the *positive* aspects of the executive's authority. This being the case, Roosevelt took up Hamilton's assertion that a president could exercise any and all governing authority that was not explicitly forbidden. To those who objected that Roosevelt was creating an autocratic executive, the new president responded that the real danger was not a *potential* autocrat in the White House, but the *proven* servants of plutocrats in Congress. Expanding presidential authority would not limit democracy, he explained, it would liberate it.

Theodore Roosevelt devoted his presidency to creating a personal and direct bond with the American people. This, however, was by no means the same as merely representing them. As their tribune or steward, he acknowledged the will of the people as the ultimate source of governing authority, but he saw as his duty the task of personally inspiring and shaping that popular will. As president, Roosevelt was determined to lead, not follow, public opinion. It is widely believed—though also disputed—that he coined the phrase *bully pulpit* to describe the platform the presidency offered for molding national sentiment. Whether or not Roosevelt actually invented the phrase, he made such extensive use of *his* bully pulpit that the concept has long been associated with him.

Roosevelt ascended that pulpit whenever he needed to create public opinion that was favorable to the passage of a piece of legislation or a policy he wanted. He also used it to influence more generally the moral, social, and political values of the nation. Most notably, he exhorted his fellow citizens to support conservation of natural resources and thereby singlehandedly elevated environmentalism to a national value.

In exploiting the bully pulpit, he did not rely exclusively on his moral authority as a president speaking directly to the people, but also shrewdly cultivated the press. He did this by frequently speaking with reporters and also by personally writing articles for publication in popular and influential periodicals. It is certain that no president before Roosevelt created a more effective partnership with journalists than he, and it is arguable that neither did any chief executive who came after him.

■

President Roosevelt had an instinctual feel for promoting his agenda effectively. Not only did he exploit the bully pulpit and the press, he also neatly packaged his domestic proposals in a single tidy box with a commonsensical and compelling label: *The Square Deal*. The concept was simple. He proposed to offer a system of policy and law that curbed the predatory abuses of capital while, in turn, protected business from the radical excesses of labor.

The "Square Deal" concept caught on not only during the Roosevelt presidency, but created a model many other chief executives would emulate. Woodrow Wilson would propose the "The New Freedom"; Franklin Roosevelt, "The New Deal"; Harry Truman, "The Fair Deal"; John F. Kennedy, "The New Frontier"; and Lyndon Johnson, "The Great Society." Yet while the Square Deal was aimed at achieving equity between capital and labor, Roosevelt is best known for his leadership in antitrust actions— beginning with his move against the railroad conglomerate known as the Northern Securities Company (1902)—and his leadership in the area of labor relations. He became the first American president to enumerate the legal rights of labor, and his mediation of an end to the anthracite coal strike of 1902, which threatened to bring a deadly winter coal famine to the nation, created a precedent for subsequent chief executives.

In no area of domestic policy was Roosevelt more passionate, more creative, and more epoch-making than in his environmental leadership. He persuaded Americans that the nation's woodlands and wilderness were a precious national heritage, a collective birthright that trumped even the sacred concept of private property. Under his administration, national parks and other protected wilderness preserves, including some 43 million acres of "national forest," were set aside and shielded wholly or in part from private ownership and commercial exploitation.

It was in large measure his conservation program that prompted Roosevelt to set yet another administrative precedent: the extensive use of executive orders as substitutes for congressional legislation. For example, when Congress moved in 1908 to transfer from the president to itself the authority to create national forests in some western states (an attempt to stop Roosevelt from putting certain water sources out of the reach of big farming and industrial interests), he wrote a series of executive orders to work around the legislation and effectively recover his authority. He used executive orders in many other legislative areas as well, issuing in seven and a half years some 1,091 of them, a sum not much short of the combined total, 1,259, compiled by all twenty-five of the presidents who had preceded him.

■

If President Roosevelt stole much congressional thunder when it came to domestic policy, he left Congress even less when it came to the conduct of foreign affairs. Barely consulting the Senate or the House, he sought to bring the United States front and center on the international stage, and, as chief executive of the nation, he intended to put himself in the lead when it came to shaping the politics of the world as a whole.

His boldest international venture was the building of the Panama Canal, which was the culmination of geopolitical strategy and actions grander than anything any president had ever before undertaken. After prevailing upon the British government to relinquish its claim to joint control of a long-projected Central American canal joining the Atlantic and the Pacific, President Roosevelt sold Congress on ratification of the Hay-Herrán Treaty with Colombia (of which Panama was then a part), giving the United States the right to build and to control a canal through a six-mile-wide strip of land across the isthmus of Panama in exchange for $10 million in cash and an annuity. When the Colombian senate reneged on the deal, Roosevelt fanned the guttering flame of a Panamanian independence movement until it took fire. Within an hour and a half of Panama's virtually bloodless break with

Colombia, the president proclaimed U.S. recognition of the new nation. Almost immediately, the Panamanian government approved the canal treaty that had been rejected by Colombia. Acting essentially alone, Theodore Roosevelt had reshaped the world politically, economically, and geographically.

While Americans almost universally greeted the Panama Canal as a great and unalloyed triumph, the response to another bold stroke of Rooseveltian diplomacy, the so-called Roosevelt Corollary to the Monroe Doctrine, was mixed.

When Venezuela defaulted on debts owed to Britain and Germany, prompting those two nations to install a naval blockade and threaten invasion, everyone—including the Venezuelan government—assumed President Roosevelt would invoke the Monroe Doctrine of 1823, whereby President James Monroe had put the nations of Europe on notice that the United States would tolerate no foreign interference in the affairs of the western hemisphere. Although the president did in fact send a naval force to observe the blockade and to act in the event of an invasion, he did not simply side with Venezuela against the European powers. Instead, on December 6, 1904, he promulgated the Roosevelt Corollary, asserting the United States' right to intervene in the economic affairs of any Latin American states that were unable or unwilling to pay their just international debts. Some saw this as a prudent assertion of U.S. leadership in the hemisphere, whereas others condemned it as an instance of outright imperialism. Regardless of the controversy, the Roosevelt Corollary, like the Monroe Doctrine itself, has been frequently invoked since as a precedent for executive action in Central and South America as well as the Caribbean.

Theodore Roosevelt's willingness to position the United States as a great world power by employing "gunboat diplomacy" against the Anglo-German blockade of Venezuela, fomenting revolution in Panama, and sometimes brandishing the "big stick" of American military might (as when, in 1907, he sent the "Great

White Fleet" of the U.S. Navy on a voyage of circumnavigation intended to impress on the nations of the world the extent of American sea power) was condemned by some as belligerent and even war mongering. He answered such accusations in *An Autobiography,* published in 1913: "When I left the Presidency, I finished seven and a half years of administration, during which not one shot had been fired against a foreign foe. We were at absolute peace, and there was no nation in the world . . . whom we had wronged, or from whom we had anything to fear." In fact, other nations turned to President Roosevelt to help them make peace. In 1905, he invited representatives from Russia and Japan to convene in the little town of Portsmouth, New Hampshire, to hammer out an end to the horrifically bloody Russo-Japanese War. On September 5, after a month of negotiation and presidential mediation, the two sides concluded the Treaty of Portsmouth. The following year, the "bellicose" Roosevelt was awarded the Nobel Peace Prize. He was the first American—and the first sitting American president (Barack Obama would become the second)—to receive it. The award came in the same year, 1906, that Roosevelt successfully mediated differences between France and Germany over Morocco at the Algeciras Conference, managing not only to peacefully preserve Moroccan independence, but also the balance of power in Europe.

■

Theodore Roosevelt served most of McKinley's second term—three and a half years—and easily won election in his own right in 1904. By this time, he was as widely known by the affectionate sobriquet "Teddy" as he was by his full name. Even more significantly, he was the first U.S. president to be identified by his initials, TR, a spontaneous popular honor that would be accorded to only a few of the strongest chief executives who followed later in the century: FDR, JFK, and LBJ. "Teddy" and "TR"—these showed that Theodore Roosevelt had established himself not just as a president but as a presidential brand, a popular icon of executive leadership. He could surely have run for another term in his own right in 1908, but he declared an unwillingness to break the two-term precedent established by George Washington. (The Twenty-second Amendment, constitutionalizing the two-term limit, would not be adopted until 1951.) Instead, he satisfied himself with handpicking his successor, William Howard Taft, who he was confident would carry forth and continue his progressive policies.

It was not long after Taft's inauguration on March 4, 1909, however, that former President Roosevelt came to understand that his faith in his successor had been misplaced. He proved a passive, reticent president who did tend to favor progressive policies but nevertheless declined to champion them. As a result, the nation (in Roosevelt's view) slid backward toward the slothful comfort of the pre-TR status quo.

Roosevelt diverted himself with a spectacular African hunting expedition spanning March 1909 to June 1910, in which he bagged many fine specimens for the Smithsonian Institution. After this, he embarked on a grand European tour and was gratified by warm and enthusiastic popular welcomes wherever he visited. On his return to the United States, he published *African Game Trails*, then reentered politics on August 31 with the delivery, in Osawatomie, Kansas, of a speech titled "New Nationalism." He continued to capture the public spotlight as editor of *Outlook Magazine* during 1911 and with a new book, *Realizable Ideals*, in 1912. Early that year, he announced that he was throwing his "hat in the ring"—an expression he is widely credited with having coined—for the Republican presidential nomination. He intended to oust William Howard Taft, the incumbent he himself had chosen.

Republican voters were enthusiastic, and TR won every caucus and primary but one. Despite this, the Republican National

Convention refused to nominate him, choosing instead to renominate President Taft on June 22. Later that summer, during August, a new third party held its first national convention in the Chicago coliseum. They called themselves the "National Progressive Party," but most people referred to them as the "Bull Moose Party." By whatever name it was known, the party chose Roosevelt as its candidate.

He campaigned vigorously against both Taft and the Democratic nominee—another man with progressive ideas, Woodrow Wilson—and looked to stand a fair chance of becoming history's first third-party candidate to be sent to the White House. The campaign very nearly came to a tragic and bloody end when, on October 14, 1912, while exiting his car to make a campaign speech in Milwaukee, candidate Roosevelt was approached by one John Schrank. The former saloon owner had had a dream in which the ghost of William McKinley bade him to shoot Theodore Roosevelt. In obedience to that nocturnal visitation, Schrank pumped a single bullet into the candidate's chest.

It should have killed him. But it did not. Although fired point-blank, the projectile was deflected by a steel eyeglass case in Roosevelt's coat pocket and then slowed further by the double-folded thick manuscript of his long speech. The slug lodged in his chest, but when he realized that he was not coughing up blood, Roosevelt concluded that the bullet was buried in muscle, not lung, and he resolved to deliver the speech, beginning by melodramatically exposing his blood-soaked shirtfront to the audience. He spoke for a full hour and a half.

"It takes more than [a bullet] to kill a Bull Moose," he announced.

Both Wilson and Taft voluntarily suspended their campaigns until Roosevelt sufficiently recovered to resume his. On election day, the Bull Moose candidate took 27.4 percent of the popular vote, bringing him in behind Wilson but ahead of Taft. If he could not claim a victory, neither did he concede a defeat.

In 1913, Roosevelt published *An Autobiography* and *History as Literature and Other Essays*, then, in October, set out on a South American lecture tour and a perilous jungle expedition sponsored jointly by the American Museum of Natural History and the government of Brazil. The objective of the trek was exploration of the South American nation's mysterious Rio da Duvida ("River of Doubt"). A bout of malaria and an infected leg injury nearly killed him. But they did not. As for the River of Doubt, it was renamed Rio Roosevelt–though some have persisted in calling it Rio Teodoro.

On his return to the States, a prematurely aged Roosevelt recuperated by writing one book, *Through the Brazilian Wilderness*, and coauthoring another, *Life-Histories of African Game Animals*. After the Great War (World War I) erupted in Europe in the summer of 1914, he published *America and the World War*, making his case for America's immediate entry into the maelstrom, which he saw as a struggle of democracy against autocracy. For the next two years, he relentlessly shamed the Wilson administration into taking the country to war; however, he turned down the Progressive Party nomination for the presidency in 1916 and instead backed mainstream Republican nominee Charles Evans Hughes. When Wilson defeated Hughes, Roosevelt resumed his pro-war campaign, and as soon as the Democratic president finally asked Congress for a declaration against Germany and the other Central Powers in April 1917, Roosevelt pleaded with him for permission to raise and lead a unit of volunteers. Wilson politely turned him down.

■

The Theodore Roosevelt of 1917 was not the Theodore Roosevelt of 1898, some two decades of "the strenuous life" having worn him down. In 1918, he published *The Great Adventure*, subtitled "*Present-Day Studies in American Nationalism*," but declined the

Republican nomination for New York governor. News that his son Quentin, flying with U.S. forces in France, had been shot down reached him in July 1918. Already struggling to recover from the lingering effects of malaria, he was overwhelmed by Quentin's loss. On the night of January 6, 1919, he fell asleep, and sometime in the next few hours suffered a coronary thrombosis. Death caught Theodore Roosevelt sleeping at last.

# Lead the Strenuous Life

## Lesson 1
## Be a Part of It

"The men who take part in [prize] fights are hard as nails, and it is not worth while to feel sentimental about their receiving punishment which as a matter of fact they do not mind. Of course the men who look on ought to be able to stand up with the gloves, or without them, themselves; I have scant use for the type of sportsmanship which consists merely in looking on at the feats of some one else."

~ *An Autobiography*, 1913

In the summer of 1872, when Roosevelt was thirteen years old, he had one of the many episodes of asthma that dogged his childhood. Having had the attack, he later wrote, "I was sent off by myself to Moosehead Lake," since it was believed that the bracing country air would do him good. "On the stage-coach ride thither, I encountered a couple of other boys who were about my own age, but very much more competent and also much more mischievous. . . . They found that I was a foreordained and predestined victim, and industriously proceeded to make life miserable for me. The worst feature was that when I finally tried to fight them I discovered that either one singly could not only handle me with easy contempt, but handle me so as not to hurt me much and yet prevent my doing any damage in return." Thoroughly humiliated by this experience, young Roosevelt resolved then and there to join what he referred to as "the fellowship of the doers." His first step was to take boxing lessons.

He would enjoy the sport, as a spectator and, far more, a participant, well into his White House years. Indeed, a blow to the face in the course of a sparring match while he was president led to the loss of sight in one eye—a fact he managed to keep secret for a long time.

Whatever the enterprise, as TR saw it, if you wanted in on it, a leadership role over it, or even just a voice in it, you had to leap in. For him, watching from the sidelines was never an option. You had to have skin in the game if you expected to derive anything from the game. This meant accepting the risks as well as anticipating the rewards; it meant enduring the pain along with the exhilaration; and it meant embracing the prospect of defeat along with the intention and the hope of victory.

> **Whatever your job title,** you cannot truly take charge without first joining "the fellowship of the doers." A leader can never be a spectator.

■

## Lesson 2
## Be Hands On

> "I cannot help thinking that the people with motor boats miss a great deal. If they would only keep to rowboats or canoes, and use oar or paddle . . . they would get infinitely more benefit than by having their work done for them by gasoline."
>
> *~ An Autobiography*, 1913

Interpreted most superficially, TR's advocacy of living what he called "the strenuous life" was about nothing more than building body and health through exercise. He was the poster boy for the concept, having overcome a childhood of chronic illness and frailty through a self-imposed regimen of strenuous "manly" physical activities, ranging from calisthenics, football, boxing, and hard riding, to hiking, climbing, and hunting, and culminating in ranching way out west.

But "the strenuous life" was also about more than this. It was about living life hands-on and doing for yourself. To lead others, TR believed you had to set a personal example, which spoke louder and clearer than mere words. To set an example, you had to learn to do for yourself and to take every opportunity to receive such life lessons. The motorboat might be modern–and Roosevelt was a "progressive" in every sense; he embraced all manner of innovative technology–but what a motorboat sailor gained in ease and speed he lost in the kind of "strenuous life" experience that builds a leader. The feel of the oar in the hands, the wearing of calluses, the building of muscle in biceps and back, the sense of the water's resistance to the paddles, the satisfying soreness of sinew after a day of rowing, the skill required to steer the boat just where you wanted it to go: all of these contributed to building a human being with the "right stuff" (that, too, was a favorite Roosevelt phrase) to wield wisely and effectively the most powerful weapon in a leader's arsenal: personal example.

**Nothing is more valuable** to leading an enterprise than continual, intimate, unmediated contact with dynamic reality. Live—and lead—hands on.

■

### Lesson 3
## Consider Resistance the Reward of Effort

> "Theodore craved the actual effort of the arms and back, the actual sense of meeting the wave close to . . . ."
> ~ Corinne Roosevelt, remarking about her teenaged brother at the oars of a rowboat, *My Brother, Theodore Roosevelt*, 1921

Living his self-invented doctrine of "the strenuous life," Theodore Roosevelt rarely missed an opportunity to exert himself. To him, effort was a privilege and a pleasure. Making your mark on the world required overcoming resistance, but far from wishing the resistance would vanish, Roosevelt welcomed it. The feeling of conquest, like the sensation of rowing—"the actual effort of the arms and back, the actual sense of meeting the wave close to"—was as great a reward as achieving the object of the conquest itself. Maybe it was even greater.

> **Accept resistance in all its forms**—disagreement, complaint, anxiety, misunderstanding—and be thankful for the opportunity resistance gives you to deliver your personal best in overcoming it. Revel in the effort.

■

### Lesson 4
## Embrace a Stronger Work Ethic

" . . . I fear he sleeps little . . ."
~Letter from Roosevelt's sister Corinne to his brother Elliott,
March 4, 1884

Just to read a bare-bones summary of New York assemblyman Roosevelt's activities from the end of February to the middle of March 1884 is an exhausting experience:

February 25, Monday: Interrogates a New York corrections officer on illegal charges for prisoner transport.

February 26, Tuesday: Urges passage of the Municipal Indebtedness Bill he has authored.

February 27, Wednesday: Works on amendments to a Bill for the Benefit of Colored Orphans; reports four bills out of the Cities Committee he chairs.

February 28, Thursday: Brings out of committee seven new bills to the Assembly.

February 29, Friday: Travels from Albany to New York City to conduct investigation of clerking procedures at Surrogate's Court, patronage at the Bureau of Citations, research fees at the Bureau of Arrears.

March 1, Saturday: Hears testimony concerning drunkenness and sex in New York city jails.

March 3, Monday: Chairs another investigative session in New York City.

March 4, Tuesday: Returned to Albany, moves banking legislation to its third reading and speaks in support of the Liquor License Bill he has authored.

March 5, Wednesday: Reports a dozen new bills out of his Cities Committee.

March 6, Thursday: Reports seven new bills out of his Cities Committee.

March 7, Friday: In New York City, commences a weekend of investigative hearings.

On Thursday, March 13, legal counsel for Roosevelt's Cities Committee delivers to him the draft of a report on the various hearings he has held. He sits down with the report and reads it in its entirety through the night. Dismissing it as a "white-washing performance," he holes up in his Albany room with 1,054 pages of testimony, which he uses to compose and dictate a new report, from scratch, using a relay of stenographers. When they give out in the wee hours of Friday morning, he continues writing the new report in his own hand and attends that day's assembly session even as he pushes on with the writing during ongoing debates (in which he manages also to participate). As he finishes each group of pages, he summons a messenger, who delivers them to the assembly's printer.

By the afternoon, Roosevelt distributes the fifteen-thousand-word report, printed and bound, to the members of the assembly. He uses it immediately as the basis for nine new bills he himself draws up.

> **The hard truth is that** there is no substitute for hard work. If your objective is to make yourself indispensable to your organization, work longer, faster, and harder than anyone else.

■

### Lesson 5
## Mix It Up

"The man who, in the long run, will count for most in bettering municipal life is the man who actually steps down into the hurly-burly, who is not frightened by the sweat and the blood, and the blows of friends and foes; who haunts not the fringy edges of the fight, but the pell-mell of men."

~ *The Outlook*, December 21, 1895

Theodore Roosevelt began his political career in 1881 as a New York State assemblyman, continued it as a member of the United States Civil Service Commission (1888–95), and came to full public prominence during 1895 to 1897, as president of the New York City Police Board, in which capacity he served, in effect, as the civilian commissioner of the city's police department.

On the day that he took the job, the NYPD was notorious as the most corrupt, brutal, and generally inept big city police department in the United States. On the day he left it, the department was the envy of every major city in the country. The journey from point A to point B took him through the nighttime streets of the slums of Manhattan. A typical night started at two in the morning when Roosevelt—sometimes alone, sometimes accompanied by a newspaperman (such as his friend, the crusading journalist Jacob

Riis) or a fellow commissioner—walked the assigned beats of the patrol cops. During many of these excursions, he found (in the words of Roosevelt biographer Edmund Morris) "that New York's Finest were also among its rarest." When he discovered two patrolmen loitering outside a liquor store instead of pounding the pavement, he approached them and demanded: "Why don't you two men patrol your posts?" Receiving a predictably angry response, he identified himself, whereupon the men scurried to their assigned beats.

Throughout it all, he took names and badge numbers. The *Excise Herald* exuberantly recorded a typical exchange in a Third Avenue "oyster saloon," complete with stage directions:

*Roosevelt (entering): Why aren't you on your post, officer?*

*[Patrolman] Rath (deliberately swallowing oyster): What the _____ is it to you?*

*Counter Man: You gotta good nerve, comin' in here and interferin' with an officer.*

*Roosevelt: I'm Commissioner Roosevelt.*

*Rath (reaching for vinegar bottle): Yes, you are. You're Grover Cleveland and Mayor Strong all in a bunch, you are. Move on now, or—*

*Counter Man (in a horrified whisper): Shut up, Bill, it's His Nibs, sure, don't you spot his glasses?*

*Roosevelt (authoritatively): Go to your post at once.*

*(EXIT patrolman, running)*

It was by walking the streets, engaging problems where and when they occurred, challenging bad behavior where and when he saw it, making his presence known not once or twice in a few months, but almost every night, that Roosevelt led—*dragged* is the more accurate word—the New York City Police Department out of the mud and elevated it to the status of national model. To be sure, during the day, he attended to administrative and legislative matters that enabled the translation of his hands-on work into disciplinary actions, rules, regulations, and laws. But at night, he threw himself into the fray, assessed front-line conditions, and asserted what military men call his "command presence" in the very faces of the troops.

> **Much of what a manager** or other executive does is administrative. This work is important and should never be evaded or slighted. But administration alone does not constitute leadership. Show yourself wherever the work is done. Get into it. Mix it up. Make your authoritative presence known. Issue clear orders and, just as important, offer support. Getting out and about like this is hard work. Commissioner Roosevelt gave up his sleep to do it.

■

## Lesson 6
## Offer Defiance

"I fight when I am attacked!"

~ Dispute in City Hall, New York, May 5, 1896

As president of the New York City Police Board, Roosevelt led a vigorous campaign against the corruption rampant in the department, particularly when it came to the department's failure to enforce certain laws, including those regulating saloons. On May 5, 1896, Commissioner Roosevelt responded with defiance when City

Comptroller Ashbel P. Fitch rejected his request for city funds to finance his campaign against illegal saloons and illegal practices by saloons.

"If we are brought to a standstill," Roosevelt, fists clenched, warned, "if we have to shut down in our work it is your fault!"

When Fitch dismissively advised him to "stop scolding" him and to seek the funding from a court, Roosevelt shot back: "You are the one to blame!"

"Tush! Tush!" Fitch replied, "I won't discuss the matter with you in this fashion. You're always looking for a fight."

"I fight when I am attacked!" Roosevelt erupted.

In the end, Commissioner Roosevelt did not get the funding he wanted, but he did win a larger following among the public, who admired his willingness to stand his ground and fight for what was right.

**Spoiling for a fight** is rarely the best way to begin a negotiation, but sometimes and at some point in the process, the integrity of your defiance is the only card you have left to play. Play it, and you may gain little or nothing in the short run, but, over time, you will find that your reputation has become increasingly bankable.

---

*Lesson 7*
## Promise Support, Demand Self-Reliance

"The worst lesson that can be taught to a man is to rely upon others and to whine over his sufferings."

~ *The Review of Reviews,* January 1897

"It is both foolish and wicked," Roosevelt wrote, "to teach the average man who is not well off that some wrong or injustice has been done him, and that he should hope for redress elsewhere than in his own industry, honesty and intelligence."

Detecting something that resembles a strong streak of Libertarianism in the champion of "the strenuous life" should come as no surprise, but that is only part of the Roosevelt approach to government. While he was convinced that democracy required every citizen to be strongly self-reliant, he also believed in a government that protected and supported every citizen. This was the essence of what he later called the "Square Deal": Every person in society should work earnestly to pull his or her own weight and, in return, would be given the support of federal law and federal regulation to help ensure that he or she would always be enabled to enjoy the fruits of self-reliance. In TR's map of good government, there were no one-way streets. All relations between citizens and their nation were mutual.

**Foster autonomy, initiative,** and self-reliance among the members of your organization, but never leave anyone out or behind. Encouragement, support, creative criticism, and assistance build the context in which people become highly productive self-starters.

■

*Lesson 8*
## Motivate Yourself

"Somehow or other I always knew that if I did not go I never would forgive myself . . ."
~Letter to Henry Cabot Lodge, July 19, 1898

Roosevelt could have named a dozen reasons for his decision to resign from the McKinley administration to risk his life fighting in the front lines of the Spanish-American War. He could have spoken of his country's call, of duty, of patriotism, of a burning desire to help the Cubans liberate themselves from Spanish cruelty, or of the necessity of making good on the Monroe Doctrine by sweeping out of the hemisphere the last vestige of European colonialism. Or he could have spoken of a hunger for the great adventure of combat. (In a fragment published in 1926 [*The Works of Theodore Roosevelt*, edited by Hermann Hagedorn], he wrote almost shockingly that "All men who feel any power of joy in battle know what it is like when the wolf rises in the heart.")

To his close friend Senator Henry Cabot Lodge, he gave no such explanations of his motive for taking up arms at the head of the Rough Riders. Instead, he confessed his knowing at the time that, if he failed to go, he would "never forgive himself."

Was it a self-centered, even selfish motive?

Perhaps. But that is really beside the point. Self-centered or selfish, the motive was first and last true, deep, certain, and utterly compelling. It was the kind of visceral basis, born of keen self-knowledge, from which Theodore Roosevelt most often acted. "I would rather have led that charge and earned my colonelcy," he wrote to his brother-in-law Theodore Douglas Robinson on July 27, 1898, "than serve three terms in the United States Senate. It makes me feel as though I could now leave something to my children which will serve as an apology to my having existed."

**If you are trained to lead**—educated to manage—you are taught to base decisions on the dispassionate analysis of facts. Such discipline has its uses, but you should never allow it to sever your connection with the much truer, deeper, more certain, and more urgently compelling sources of motivation within yourself. Faced with an especially difficult decision, ask how you will feel if you act one way or the other. Imagine that feeling. Then, having imagined it vividly, make your choice.

[ 35 ]

## Lesson 9
## Fighting Words

"Don't hit at all if you can help it; don't hit a man if you can possibly avoid it; but if you do hit him, put him to sleep."
~Speech, National Press Club, Washington, D.C., January 24, 1918

"Now look!" Senator Mark Hanna of Ohio groaned when news reached him that William McKinley had succumbed to gunshot wounds inflicted a week earlier by assassin Leon Czolgosz. "That damned cowboy is president of the United States!"

Hanna was not alone in his fear that Vice President—now President—Theodore Roosevelt would prove to be a violently impulsive leader. Like these others, Hanna made the common mistake of equating TR's bigger-than-life presence, his overpowering aura of limitless energy, his commanding voice, and his air of absolute self-assurance with snap decisions and thoughtless acts. Roosevelt was, in fact, a deliberative leader, who thoroughly researched each major decision before he made it, and who sought from those around him lively debate and disagreement. Invariably, however, once he had reached a decision, action followed both quickly and decisively. Slow to strike, he made certain, when he did strike, to strike without a trace of ambivalence or ambiguity. Long restrained, when the blow came it was a knockout.

**Every decision has at** least two phases, which must be kept separate and distinct. The first phase is the formulation of the decision. The best decisions are typically products of study, research, deliberation, discussion, soul searching, and debate. This takes time and frequently requires numerous changes of course. The process of making a decision is often the very picture of indecision. This is not only normal, it is a sign of sound decision making.

The second phase is the point at which the decision is put

into action. This phase cannot be permitted to begin until the first phase is absolutely ended. Movement from the first to the second phase is strictly one way. There can be no going back. Once a decision is put into action, debate must end—at least until results are produced.

Deliberate before you strike. Review and revise your plan of attack. Avoid unnecessary action. But once you put a decision into action, resolve to score nothing less than a knockout.

■

*Lesson 10*
## Preach the Strenuous Life (and Practice It, Too)

"I wish to preach, not the doctrine of ignoble ease, but the doctrine of the strenuous life."

~Speech to the Hamilton Club, Chicago, April 10, 1899

Fast-forward to more than six decades after Theodore Roosevelt, horseman, boxer, hiker, mountain climber, rancher, and vice president of the United States, announced his intention to preach "the doctrine of the strenuous life." It was April 12, 1961, just over three months into the term of John F. Kennedy, the youngest president of the United States since TR. That day, news came that the Soviet Union, having beaten America into space four years earlier with the unmanned satellite *Sputnik I,* had just orbited Cosmonaut Yuri Gagarin, the first man in space.

Americans, who had built the world's greatest economy and had mightily prevailed in two world wars, were suddenly looking like the losers in a space race that pitted a communist society against a democratic one. Inside the Kennedy administration, there were calls to cut our losses by ditching the whole manned space program in favor of developing and launching unmanned general science, communications, and military satellites. In practical terms, the advice made good sense, but Kennedy rejected it nonetheless, reasoning that the American people and the entire world were judging the merits of the Soviet Union and the United States by their achievements. In terms of science, commerce, and tactical military utility, specialized unmanned satellites would be very significant achievements. But in human terms, as measured by minds persuaded and hearts won, nothing spoke more powerfully of mastery than putting human beings beyond the Earth.

The president conceded that the Soviets had won the first laps of the space race, and there would be no rerunning them. Instead, he decided to begin a new race, a contest that would capture and hold the imagination of the entire world. Kennedy decided to go to the moon.

He broached this to Congress on May 25, 1961: "I believe that this nation should commit itself to achieving the goal, before this decade is out, of landing a man on the Moon and returning him safely to the Earth. No single space project in this period will be more impressive to mankind, or more important for the long-range exploration of space; and none will be so difficult or expensive to accomplish." At this time, America had done nothing more than send Astronaut Alan B. Shepard on a fifteen-minute suborbital flight, an achievement that paled in comparison to Gagarin's multiple orbits.

On September 12, 1962, Kennedy showed how well he understood the meaning of "difficult" and "expensive." Speaking to the students and faculty of Rice University, he proclaimed, "We choose to go to the moon. We choose to go to the moon in this decade and do the other things, not because they are easy, but because they are hard, because that goal will serve to organize and measure the best of our energies and skills, because that challenge is one that we are willing to accept, one we are unwilling to postpone, and one which we intend to win, and the others, too."

The worth of the goal was directly proportional to its difficulty.

Sixty-two years after Vice President Roosevelt's speech in Chicago, JFK had reasserted the value of "the strenuous life" and projected it on an international scale.

> **"A man's reach should exceed his grasp,"** the poet Robert Browning wrote. Theodore Roosevelt called this the doctrine of "the strenuous life." John F. Kennedy used his version of the doctrine to send America to the moon.
> What can you achieve if you lead your enterprise in things not because they are easy but because they are hard?

■

*Lesson 11*
## Dare

"Far better it is to dare mighty things, to win glorious triumphs, even though checkered by failure, than to take rank with those poor spirits who neither enjoy much nor suffer much, because they live in the gray twilight that knows not victory nor defeat."
~ Speech to the Hamilton Club, Chicago, April 10, 1899

Demanding greatness *from* America, Roosevelt resolved to impose greatness *on* it by his own example. He believed in aiming high. He believed that risking failure always had a greater upside than downside because the risk itself was a powerful tonic to the spirit. He deemed aspiration, not just achievement, to be in itself a positive good.

The Roosevelt agenda was less about creating a set of externally tangible results than it was about building an internal spiritual and intellectual national identity—a passion for attempting great things. He therefore emphasized the striving even more than the fruits of that arduous process. The fight, provided it was a good fight, a fight fought in good faith, was of greater value than any victory it might produce. And if it resulted in a defeat, the value of the fight—again, provided it was a good one—outweighed the loss by far. Roosevelt cared less for growing the United States than he did for developing the American people.

**Encourage, cajole, goad, and demand** greatness from the members of your enterprise. In the short term, this may produce failures, and you and your organization will have to pay the costs of those failures. But in the long run, striving always higher is a mental and spiritual orientation that creates greatness in any collaborative endeavor. And, in the long run, greatness has a far better chance of creating profitable success than what you may expect from remaining in the gray mediocrity of twilight.

■

**Lesson 12**
## Lead the Strenuous Life—and More

"It is a good thing for a boy to have captained his school or college eleven, but it is a very bad thing if, twenty years afterward, all that can be said of him is that he has continued to take an interest in football, baseball, or boxing, and has with him the memory that he was once captain."

~ "Character and Success," *The Outlook*, March 31, 1900

Although Roosevelt preached lifelong the virtues of "the strenuous life," feats of physical fitness by no means topped his hierarchy of values. "Athletics are good," he advised in an address to the Harvard Union on February 23, 1907, but "study is even better; and best of all is the development of the type of character for the lack of which, in an individual as in a nation, no amount of brilliancy of mind or of strength of body will atone."

TR boxed in the White House and went on safari after he left it. He never gave up "the strenuous life." He felt that unflagging maximum effort kept him young—as his friend Cecil Spring-Rice observed, "You must remember that the President is about six"—and it is therefore no surprise that he himself associated physical sport and athletic competition with childhood and youth. These activities were necessary in adulthood, he believed, but hardly sufficient in themselves to create the achievements of maturity. A wonderful thing to be captain of the school football team, but inadequate to fill, let alone justify, the many years of a lifetime that follow graduation.

To understand Theodore Roosevelt's hierarchy of personal values, you might paraphrase what Saint Paul preached in his First Epistle to the Corinthians: And now abideth the *strenuous life, study, character*, these three; but the greatest of these is character. Develop and demonstrate character, and you will of necessity broadcast it through every level of your organization.

■

*Lesson 13*
## Offer All You Have

"I am as strong as a bull moose and you can use me to the limit."
~ Reply, on June 17, 1900, to Republican Party leader Senator Mark Hanna of Ohio in answer to his request that he serve as William McKinley's running mate in the 1900 presidential election

"The strenuous life" was not just a regime of physical exertion. For Theodore Roosevelt, it was a philosophy of conduct and commitment. It was an expression of his disdain for half-measures and half-hearted responses. For TR, decision making was essentially a binary process, not a complex calculation. Either a contemplated action was worth taking or it was not. If it was worth taking, then the endeavor both merited and required maximum effort. If he believed himself incapable of summoning up such an effort, he rejected the proposal.

This did not mean that Roosevelt made snap decisions. Quite the contrary. Offered the vice presidency, he agonized over the decision, weighing the pros and cons painstakingly before he decided to accept. Once he made that decision, the binary switch was thrown from 0 to 1, the only two possible positions, and he did not hesitate to put absolutely everything he had into the effort.

> **Simplify decision making** by asking yourself the Rooseveltian question: *If I agree to this, am I willing to be used to the limit?* Your decision is thereby reduced to yes or no. When people learn that when you say yes to them you will give all that you have, they will value your integrity, your heart, and your strength. They will be powerfully inclined to respond accordingly and in kind.

■

### Lesson 14
## Self-Reliance: The Ultimate Test

> "Excepting in a crowd I do not think a bodyguard is the least use....
> [I]f there is any chance to break even with a would-be assassin I
> think the man himself, if alert and resolute, has a better opportunity
> to defend himself than any bodyguard would have to defend him."
> ~Letter to William H. H. Llewellyn, former Rough Rider under
> Roosevelt's command, October 19, 1901

Vice President Theodore Roosevelt became the twenty-sixth president of the United States on September 14, 1901, when the twenty-fifth, William McKinley, succumbed to wounds inflicted eight days earlier by Leon Czolgosz, an unemployed factory worker who had turned anarchist after hearing a speech by the radical Emma Goldman.

On the afternoon of September 6, 1901, Czolgosz had wrapped his right hand in a white handkerchief to hide the revolver he carried with him into the Temple of Music at the Pan-American Exposition in Buffalo, New York. In that building, he found a place in a line of well-wishers eager to shake hands with President McKinley, who was attending a "President's Day" reception at the exposition. At precisely 4:07 p.m., Czolgosz extended what appeared to be a bandaged hand. The president reached out to shake it. The assassin—for that is what the jobless man was now about to become—fired two shots. One round was deflected by a rib, but the other tore into McKinley's stomach, grazed his kidney, gouged his pancreas, and then lodged in the muscles of his back. Doctors probed in vain for the bullet, doubtless hastening the onset of the infection that would end his life.

The new president, Roosevelt, ordered no special investigation of the police and president's guards. He placed no blame on anyone but Czolgosz himself—though, perhaps, wordlessly and by implication, he also faulted the victim, William McKinley. Concerning attack from behind, Roosevelt was fatalistic and accepted the fact that he would "go down into the darkness," but if he were approached as McKinley had been, from the front, he believed that his finely tuned reflexes would serve him well as would his 185-pound fighter's body. In fact, as he explained to his former Spanish-American War comrade-at-arms William H. H. Llewellyn, bodyguards would only interfere with his capacity to defend himself. Face to face with an armed assassin, TR accepted the odds of self-reliance. Throughout his presidency—and during an era in which "anarchists" loomed in the American psyche much as al-Qaeda terrorists do today—Roosevelt even looked forward to the prospect of such an encounter, face to face, as the ultimate test of his self-reliance.

> **By definition, leadership is** never a solo act. Yet so that others may rely on her, a leader must above all possess the highest possible degree of *self*-reliance. All that a leader says and does must be said and done with an eye toward those she leads. Yet the core of leadership—the point at which the decision process becomes a decision, the moment at which a decision becomes action—must be entirely self-built, requiring no support from the outside.

■

### Lesson 15
## Work

"I have never won anything without hard labor and the exercise of my best judgment and careful planning and working long in advance."

~Speech, Des Moines, Iowa, November 4, 1910

Few men have loved their lives more than Teddy Roosevelt. Whether it was hunting, writing, or championing legislation, he approached his work with zeal and a sense of total joy. Yet if anyone had dared tell him that he led a charmed life, he would surely have snapped back that "charm" had nothing at all to do with it. The success, the joy, the intensity of passion were all the products of "hard labor" and long work.

We do not know how his Des Moines audience received his remarks. We cannot answer the question of how they felt when they learned that TR and all that he had become were the products of hard labor, judgment, careful planning, and long advance work. Were they disappointed because the speaker revealed no shortcut secret to success? Or were they encouraged to learn that the old virtues, commonplace as they are, could, if diligently applied, yield extraordinary results? We do not know, but we can look to the example of Theodore Roosevelt as proof that hard work can and does bring rich reward.

> **"Work smart," we're often** advised, "not hard." The example of Teddy Roosevelt suggests that working hard *is* working smart. How you respond—with chagrin or with satisfaction—to the workaday revelation that there are no substitutes for really hard work, very long work, and tediously careful planning is entirely up to you.

■

### Lesson 16
## Try

> "Life is a great adventure, and I want to say to you, accept it in such a spirit. I want to see you face it ready to do the best that lies in you to win out; and resolute, if you do not win out, to go down without complaining, doing the best that is in you, and abiding the results."
> ~Speech, Occidental College, Los Angeles, March 22, 1911

*Win* is the exhortation of a football coach. Roosevelt dearly loved football, but he knew, in the end, it was just a game, whereas life was an adventure. His exhortation for living life was not, therefore, to *win* but to *fight*, to *strive*, to *revel*, and to *try*. The effort you made was everything. Give it your best, and you can abide the results, whatever they are.

> **In the end,** you can influence but not determine the result of any endeavor. You can, however, resolve to deliver your best effort relentlessly and always. Since no one can do more, this in itself defines true victory, regardless of outcome.

## Lesson 17
## Accept the Cost of Doing Business

"I did not care a rap for being shot. It is a trade risk, which every prominent public man ought to accept as a matter of course. For eleven years I have been prepared any day to be shot."

~Letter to his friend Cecil Spring-Rice, December 31, 1912

John Flammang Schrank was born in 1876 in Bavaria and was taken to America by his parents when he was just three years old. Orphaned shortly after the family arrived in the country, Schrank went to live with and work for his uncle, who owned a tavern in New York City. When his uncle and aunt died years later, he inherited the tavern and an apartment building. It was a stroke of fortune that should have afforded Schrank a comfortable living, but the deaths of his adoptive parents and of his own sweetheart soon afterward left him a heartbroken drifter who turned to religion, Bible study, and the writing of poetry for solace.

Sometime prior to October 14, 1912, when Theodore Roosevelt came to Milwaukee, Wisconsin, during his Progressive Party campaign for the presidency, the melancholy Schrank had a dream (he later reported) in which he was visited by the ghost of President William McKinley. Pointing to a photograph of TR, the specter told Schrank to kill him.

The unhinged man shadowed the campaigning Roosevelt from New Orleans to Milwaukee. He read in a local paper that the candidate was scheduled to attend a dinner at the Gilpatrick Hotel before delivering a speech at the Milwaukee Auditorium. Schrank went to the hotel and waited outside. When Roosevelt, having finished his dinner, walked out the front doors to enter his waiting car, Schrank fired a revolver at pointblank range into his chest.

The round lodged in the flesh and muscle of his broad chest, having been substantially slowed as it passed through both his steel eyeglass case and the twice-folded, fifty-page manuscript of his speech.

The former president knew he had been shot. He knew the bullet was in his chest. But he noted with relief that he was not coughing up blood and therefore concluded that the projectile had not penetrated his lung. Over the strident objections of everyone around him, he firmly refused to be driven to the hospital, insisting instead on delivering his speech.

It was a performance of the highest drama.

"Friends," he began, "I shall ask you to be as quiet as possible. I don't know whether you fully understand that I have just been shot; but it takes more than that to kill a Bull Moose. But fortunately I had my manuscript, so you see I was going to make a long speech, and there is a bullet . . ." At this he opened his coat and vest to reveal his blood-drenched shirtfront. "There is where the bullet went through, and it [the manuscript] probably saved me from it going into my heart. The bullet is in me now, so that I cannot make a very long speech, but I will try my best."

He spoke, in point of fact, for ninety minutes. Throughout, several times, he impatiently waved off entreaties that he stop and go to the hospital.

"Don't you waste any sympathy on me," he said. "I have had an A–1 time in life and I am having it now."

When he finally finished, ambulance attendants approached him with a stretcher.

"I'll not go to the hospital lying in that thing," he snapped. "I'll walk to it [the ambulance] and I'll walk from it to the hospital. I'm no weakling to be crippled by a flesh wound."

At the hospital, the attending physicians were inclined to agree with Roosevelt's assessment of the relatively minor nature of his wound. They decided to leave the bullet where it was rather than risk enlarging the injury by probing for it. Out of respect for Roosevelt as well as a sense of gentlemanly fair play, both of his opponents, Democratic candidate Woodrow Wilson and

Republican nominee William Howard Taft, the incumbent, ceased campaigning until Roosevelt recovered sufficiently to resume his campaign.

Roosevelt never complained about the bullet he carried with him to the grave, once commenting that he did "not mind it anymore than if it were in my waistcoat pocket." Nor did he ask for vengeance upon Schrank, who, in 1914, was committed to the Central State Mental Hospital in Waupun, Wisconsin, where he remained until his own death in 1943.

**Having succeeded to the presidency** after the assassination of William McKinley, Theodore Roosevelt was continually aware that the possibility of being shot was "a trade risk" of public life. He believed that his own acceptance of the risk should serve as an example not only to public figures but to anyone in every trade. All should understand the inevitable risks of what they do. Accept them. Prepare for them as best you can. Never whine about them.

■

*Lesson 18*
## Make Collaboration Conditional

> "All for each, and each for all, is a good motto, but only on condition that each works with might and main to so maintain himself as not to be a burden to others."
>
> ~ *An Autobiography*, 1913

As the leader of a nation and, later, of a political movement, Theodore Roosevelt proved that you could be a self-reliant individualist without becoming a lone wolf or a hermit. A president and a politician, he of course had no choice but to collaborate with a great many people. Yet he always predicated the collaboration on the condition that everyone involved had first and foremost to pull his own weight.

**The object of collaboration** is to create a synergy by which the effort the group produces is inevitably greater than the sum of the individual efforts that contributed to it. To lead a successful collaboration, you must ensure that no individual contributes less than what is required to keep him from becoming "a burden to others." To the degree that the group is obliged to carry one of its members, synergy suffers. Do not rely on creating a tide that lifts all boats. Each person must contribute to the rising tide from which each—and the group—benefits. Adhere to this requirement ruthlessly, relentlessly, and without exception.

■

## *Lesson 19*
## Pay the Price

"The things that will destroy America are prosperity-at-any-price, peace-at-any-price, safety-first instead of duty first, the love of soft living and the get-rich-quick theory of life."
~Remarks published in the *Proceedings of the Congress of Constructive Patriotism*, January 1917

For TR, only the hard-won achievements were worth their high price, whereas the easy goals generally led to decay and destruction. Prosperity-at-any-price, peace-at-any-price, safety-first instead of duty first . . . these were all disastrous bargains because they required no meaningful stake in outcomes and forsook all ethical considerations. Investment—of time, of mind, of muscle, of heart, of life itself—endowed an endeavor with value even as it forced the striver to choose only what was of genuine value.

**Beware the free lunch** and the unbelievable bargain. Effort required, a high level of difficulty, and significant risk are the best indicators of the worth of a proposed goal. If you are in doubt about what path of many to choose, always choose the hardest.

■

# Lead the
# Learning
# Life

*Lesson 20*
## A Child Shall Teach You

"Children are better than books."

~ *An Autobiography*, 1913

Teddy Roosevelt was delighted by children, and children took to him naturally and irresistibly. He felt in them a guileless enthusiasm that was not only thoroughly charming but highly instructive because (as he saw it) it stripped away the veneer of social convention, pretense, and outright deception that colors so much of adult life, leaving only the truth of human behavior and motivation. Both as entertainment and instruction, children were far better teachers than books.

**Your business is people:** persuading them, satisfying them, motivating them. Learn your business from every encounter with everyone, paying special attention to the children.

■

*Lesson 21*
## Greatness in Fact

"Tolstoi is a great writer. Do you notice how he never comments on the actions of his personages? He relates what they thought or did without any remark whatever as to whether it was good or bad, as Thucydides wrote history—a fact which tends to give his work an unmoral rather than an immoral tone."

~Letter to his sister Corinne, 1884

While he was on his ranch in Dickinson, Dakota Territory, young Roosevelt read even more voraciously than usual. Among the books he consumed was *Anna Karenina*, Leo Tolstoy's great study of passion, passionlessness, and adultery in a society alienated from meaningful values.

Roosevelt was at first troubled by the author's unwillingness to take a moral stand on the behavior of his characters, but he soon came to realize that this refusal to comment "on the actions of his personages" constituted the very stuff of Tolstoy's greatness as a writer. He wrote fiction "as Thucydides wrote history," dispassionately chronicling what his characters "thought or did" and leaving it to the reader to assess and, if necessary, condemn them—as the reader would evaluate any flesh-and-blood person—rather than tell the reader to think of a character as "good or bad."

That Theodore Roosevelt, who had grown up in a morally conventional American Victorian household and whose own personal morality tended lifelong toward the straitlaced, recognized Tolstoy's greatness in the writer's ability to see beyond convention by *showing* fact rather than *telling* interpretation is a testament as much to TR's intelligence as it is to the Russian novelist's genius.

Different as Roosevelt was from Leo Tolstoy, the two had a key quality in common. They respected fact and sought to understand rather than distort it through interpretation. If a fact was disagreeable, it was not to be ignored, shunned, or lied about, but engaged and, if necessary, changed—changed *in fact*, not in fantasy.

> **Find the truth.** Face the truth. And if the unvarnished truth is unacceptable, understand that varnishing it will not alter its essence. You must lead the change to a different truth. Merely "spinning" reality is never a sustainable leadership option.

**Lesson 22**

OJT

"One learns fast in a fight."

~ *An Autobiography*, 1913

A scholar and voracious reader—he read at least one book a day, even when he was busiest—who relished the company of other highly educated men and women, Theodore Roosevelt believed in lifelong preparation for public service. "The man with a university education," he wrote in the *Atlantic Monthly* in August 1894, "is in honor bound to take an active part in our political life. . . ." Yet he also thought that the most efficient and effective form of education came on the job itself.

Combat accelerated learning.

The richer the reward, the more dire the risk. The higher the stakes, the greater the pressure—and the faster the required lessons were learned.

**OJT—on-the-job training**—is traditionally viewed as a fallback option and, more often than not, a desperate make-do fallback at that. Managers like Roosevelt, however, saw OJT as a positive force, an invaluable accelerant to learning.

To avoid resorting to OJT in unplanned desperation, refuse to think of it as a fallback. Instead, purposely design OJT into your organization by providing backup support for everyone you throw into the fight.

**Lesson 23**
## Turn from Books to the Book of Life

> "No man ever really learned from books how to manage a
> governmental system. . . . If he has never done anything but study
> books he will not be a statesman at all."
>
> ~ In the *Atlantic Monthly*, August 1894

Theodore Roosevelt had a passion for books. He read not merely
voraciously but omnivorously, and from a life crowded with politics,
hunting, exploration, administration, statesmanship, and the cause
of conservation, he managed to extract the equivalent literary
output of a full-time professional author, writing some thirty-seven
full-length books and innumerable articles. As much as he loved
books, TR understood their limitations. Reading, he believed, could
not take the place of actually doing. He advised those who would
undertake to lead others to turn from books to the book of life: to
observe people, to work with them, and to learn from them.

Yet while he advised turning from books, he never turned
against them. In fact, if life was the best "book" for a leader to "read,"
it was also important for the "statesman . . . the publicist . . . the
reformer, and the agitator for new things" as well as "the upholder of
what is good in old things . . . to know human nature, to know the
needs of the human soul; and they will find this nature and these
needs set forth nowhere else but in the great imaginative writers,
whether of prose or poetry."

In Roosevelt's view, books of instruction, intended to be
"practical," were of limited use in teaching one "to manage a
governmental system"—that is, to lead. Better, far better, to plunge in
and learn from life itself. Yet even this—life lived—was insufficient.
Roosevelt proposed to direct would-be leaders to another shelf of
books: not the dry manuals of statesmanship and administration—
books of instruction—but the works of the "great imaginative
writers," men and women who had drawn their books from the
book of life. In these works was to be found the distillation of

human nature and human needs, of motives, desires, and fears. In these books was to be found life interpreted.

Theodore Roosevelt was a man of action *and* scholarship. He never accepted the superficial proposition that the two were mutually exclusive. On the contrary, he believed these modes of living to be mutually enriching, and he was never shy about offering himself as an example to others.

> **An effective leader** always leads toward productive action. In this he must be guided by an understanding of human nature and human needs. Such an understanding is a synthesis of personal observation and experience enlightened by the collected and varied insights of the "great imaginative writers." These are the authors who are capable of inspiring the kind and quality of thought that enables the wisest, most effective, and most productive action.

*Lesson 24*
## Practice Courage

> "Man does in fact become fearless by sheer dint of practicing fearlessness."
>
> ~ *An Autobiography*, 1913

Many popular legends surround the life of Theodore Roosevelt, but one of the most pervasive also happens to be a fact. The boy was born with a host of afflictions, including, most prominently, severe chronic asthma and what was at the time called "cholera morbus"— chronic and debilitating diarrhea. As a consequence, he grew up sickly and scrawny. The reasonable course would have been for him to resign himself to his apparent genetic destiny. His family was wealthy, and he could have embarked on a life of genteel invalidism, becoming what Victorian writers liked to call a "valetudinarian." Instead of pursuing this expected route, he resolved to take a radical detour by building up his body in an effort to acquire what he had not been born with: robust health. He therefore embarked on a largely self-designed course of hard physical exercise and intense activity, the formula for living he later dubbed "the strenuous life."

Building physical strength, transforming skin and bones into muscle, willing himself into a state of physical vigor were key goals of his program. There was, however, even more. His naturally frail state had made him something of a fearful lad. Profoundly dissatisfied with living scared, he seems to have approached the acquisition of courage in much the same way as he approached the acquisition of muscle, physical prowess, and good health. Naturally timorous, TR became fearless "by sheer dint of practicing fearlessness."

Theodore Roosevelt emerged in his own time and stands in history as that most American of American archetypes: the self-made man. Most commonly, that phrase refers to someone who achieved financial success without having been born into money. In the case of TR, however, "self-made" needs to be applied as broadly, as deeply, and as literally as possible. He saw what he was born with, he understood where nature was taking him, and, finding destiny disagreeable, he took hard, practical steps to alter it. In remaking who he was, he made who he would become.

**Courage is a coveted** leadership quality. If you don't have it, get it. Walk into situations that scare you. *Feel* the fear, but practice *acting* with courage. Practice often enough and hard enough, and you may find yourself suddenly transformed into a courageous leader.

Unsatisfied with who you are? Then remake yourself. As Theodore Roosevelt both discovered and demonstrated, it can be done—with plenty of practice.

**Lesson 25**

## Lesson from the Rough Riders

> "The only way to get them to do it in the way it had to be done
> was to lead them myself."
>
> ~Letter to his sister Corinne, July 19, 1898

Theodore Roosevelt, a passionate advocate for going to war against Spain over the issue of Cuban independence, was serving as assistant secretary of the navy when President William McKinley asked Congress for a declaration of war in 1898. Roosevelt promptly resigned his administrative post and joined forces with U.S. Army colonel Leonard Wood to recruit 1,250 men for the 1st U.S. Volunteer Cavalry Regiment. Except as a naval administrator, Roosevelt had no military experience and had never heard a shot fired in anger. He did, however, possess a sharp thirst for hazardous adventure, and his few years as a rancher in the Badlands had taught him the fighting virtues and riding prowess of the Western cowboy. Thus he set about recruiting cowboys and also filled out the unit's ranks with a selection of hunters, prospectors, and gamblers, as well as Indians and former "Buffalo soldiers"–African-American cavalry troopers–in addition to a handful of eager college boys from the East Coast Ivy League.

Roosevelt was determined to mold this raw material into a crack cavalry regiment. The popular press was instantly won over and dubbed the 1st USV the "Rough Riders," a nickname that TR and his men embraced.

Roosevelt bowed to Wood's professional military experience and accepted appointment as lieutenant colonel under him. Officially, the Rough Riders was one regiment in the 1st Cavalry Brigade, consisting of two regular army units–the 1st U.S. Cavalry and 106th U.S. Cavalry–in addition to the 1st U.S.V. Cavalry. The brigade was commanded by a general, but when he fell ill with yellow fever, Wood was promoted to brigade command and Roosevelt, bumped up to colonel, took over the Rough Riders.

Both Wood and Roosevelt insisted that the Rough Riders, independent and even motley though they were, would receive full standard military training, including liberal helpings of drill and lessons in strict military courtesy. Roosevelt agreed, however, that, unlike the men of the regular U.S. cavalry, the Rough Riders would forgo saber training and instead drill with the weapons they knew best: carbines and revolvers. Second in command though he was, Roosevelt trained alongside his men—in part to set an example for them, and in part to learn all that he knew he had to learn. When he was not in the saddle, Colonel Roosevelt devoured books on tactics and strategy, trying to cram the equivalent of four years of West Point into a few weeks of training.

Roosevelt quickly shaped himself into a seasoned—albeit instantly seasoned—commander. He absorbed and practiced cavalry fighting techniques and he force-fed himself the art of war. Most of all, he learned and he led by direct example.

He could not use everything he learned. When it came to the fighting—including the two central actions of the land war in Cuba, the charges up Kettle Hill and San Juan Hill (or Heights) on July 1, 1898, Roosevelt was the only Rough Rider who actually had a horse to ride. Due to the army's poor logistical planning and an acute shortage of transport, the 1st USV had had to leave all its horses on the mainland. They marched and they fought, therefore, not as cavalrymen but as infantry (and were therefore nicknamed "Wood's Weary Walkers"). Forced to fight in a manner very different from the way he and his men had trained, Roosevelt discovered in himself a genius for improvisation and for leading others in improvisation. The battles at Kettle Hill and San Juan Hill were violent, costly, and triumphant.

In depriving the Spanish of tactically critical high ground, the battles were decisive. They were also the bloodiest actions of the war, resulting in 205 men killed in action and 1,180 wounded. The Spanish, though defeated, suffered just 58 killed and 170 wounded. Colonel Roosevelt was always generous in giving his men all the credit for the victory. Yet without Roosevelt there would probably have been no assault to begin with; the operation was the product of Roosevelt's initiative, and the charges, valiant and victorious, were made without orders from any higher commander. Moreover, everyone who served under him testified to the galvanizing effect of his unfailingly heroic example.

Celebrated throughout America as a hero, Roosevelt was nominated for the Medal of Honor. That he did *not* receive it turns out to be testimony to the ongoing intensity of his identification with his men. The most appalling fact of what John Hay (at the time U.S. ambassador to Great Britain) called "the splendid little war" was that most of the casualties occurred after the shooting had stopped. Roosevelt recognized that malaria and other diseases were killing more troops than had died in battle, and he led a group of fellow officers in hurling urgent demands that the army be sent home without further delay. He was unsparing in his criticism of the War Department for failing to act expeditiously in preserving brave soldiers from epidemic disease. The press got wind of his vitriolic communications and published them. Doubtless, this helped get the boys back home faster than they otherwise would have; but it also enraged Secretary of War Russell Alger. It is generally believed that Alger quashed his Medal of Honor prospects.

The award *was* conferred, posthumously, in 2001, but the greater honor was—and remains—Colonel Roosevelt's commitment to the men for whom he was determined always to serve as an example.

**Mentor the members of** your organization—not from behind a desk, but at *their* desks, face to face with *them*. Learn as you teach. See the business from their perspective. Identify with them. Teach them to charge by leading the charge.

■

*Lesson 26*
## Grasp Opportunity

"Master of human destinies am I!"

~From "Opportunity," President Roosevelt's favorite poem,

framed opposite his desk

Born in Middleton, Massachusetts, in 1833 and an 1855 graduate of Williams College in his home state, John James Ingalls was a poet and politician who, after moving to Kansas Territory on the eve of the Civil War, worked successfully to bring the territory into the Union as a Free State. Elected to the U.S. Senate in 1873, he served until 1891, finding time to write poetry as he served the people of Kansas and the United States. One of his poems became a TR favorite. The president framed it and hung it within view of his desk:

*Opportunity*
*Master of human destinies am I!*
*Fame, love and fortune on my footsteps wait.*
*Cities and fields I walk; I penetrate*
*Deserts and seas remote, and passing by*
*Hovel and mart and palace, soon or late*
*I knock unbidden once at every gate!*
*If sleeping, wake; if feasting, rise before*
*I turn away. It is the hour of fate,*
*And they who follow me reach every state*
*Mortals desire, and conquer every foe*
*Save death; but those who doubt or hesitate,*
*Condemned to failure, penury and woe,*
*Seek me in vain and uselessly implore.*
*I answer not, and I return no more!*

**TR spoke rarely of** luck but often of opportunity. As he well knew, opportunity is something that appears only to vanish unless it is quickly recognized, seized, and exploited. It is a blessing that the majority who miss opportunity never realize it; for those who miss it and know they missed it are condemned to the keen bitterness of a regret that may well last a lifetime.

On behalf of your enterprise as well as for yourself, emulate the life stance of Theodore Roosevelt: head on a swivel, eyes wide open, poised on your toes, heart ready, mind ready, hands ready to grasp opportunity as it flashes and before it fades.

■

*Lesson 27*
## Catch the Reading Disease

> "Reading, with me, is a disease."
> ~ Quoted by J. A. Zahm in "Theodore Roosevelt
> as a Hunter-Naturalist," 1919

Even when he was at his busiest, Theodore Roosevelt invariably read a book a day. Asked what he was reading, more often than not, he would answer by delivering a concise summary, including relevant quotations. His friend the novelist Owen Wister once lent him a book just before a White House dinner, stayed in the executive mansion overnight, and was then regaled at breakfast early the next morning with the president's detailed review. "Somewhere between six one evening and eight-thirty the next morning," Wister later wrote, "beside his dressing and his dinner and his guests and his sleep, he had read a volume of three-hundred-and-odd pages, and missed nothing of significance that it contained."

Roosevelt was not only an insatiable reader and a fast reader, he was an unabashedly omnivorous reader, resolutely refusing to specialize in any particular field or genre. As the biographer Edmund Morris observed, his reading ranged from "the *Histories of Thucydides* to the *Tales of Uncle Remus*," resulting in "a continuous process of cross-fertilization . . . in his mind."

> **Roosevelt believed that** the president of the United States needed to command a vast body of knowledge. For that matter, he believed that the same requirement applied to any *citizen* of the country. As leader of your enterprise, you need to be extraordinarily well informed, not only about your company, but your industry, the larger marketplace in which it functions, and the world that marketplace occupies. Moreover, you need to demand that every member of your organization get informed, stay informed, and share the information. When it comes to acquiring knowledge, become an omnivore. Expose yourself at every opportunity to infection by the reading disease.

■

## Lesson 28
## Listen Actively

> "I need your advice and counsel."
>
> ~ At his first cabinet meeting, September 20, 1901

Sworn in on September 14, 1901, after the death of William McKinley, President Roosevelt convened his first cabinet meeting six days later. He began the meeting by asserting himself in no uncertain terms, explaining that he needed everyone to resign so that he could officially reappoint them all. He did not *ask* the secretaries to stay on, he told them that they *must*: "I cannot accept a declination." Then he added, directly but also humbly: "I need your advice and counsel."

In turn, each man began to give what the president had asked for. Anyone who expected the new chief executive to sit passively and listen, as if taking dictation, quickly discovered how mistaken he was. As with everything else he did, Theodore Roosevelt was intensely active in the way he listened. He asked many questions, and he drew out instructive detail from every briefing. His interruptions did not disrupt the flow of information, but increased it. The cabinet members were astounded by the facility with which Roosevelt took in, processed, and grasped what they told him.

**From childhood,** most of us are told many times to "listen quietly." Inevitably, we ourselves unconsciously translate this as an injunction to "listen passively." It is a terrible mistake to do so. Passive listening severely compromises the process of communication. When two people talk about something important—a topic entailing risk and reward, hazard and opportunity—much more than a transfer of information must take place. There needs to be an active creation, transmission, and processing of information, which stimulates feedback that, in turn, creates more information. The person who does the most talking—gives a report, for example—has the most obviously active role, but if you are the listener, you must listen like a leader. This means that you must be at least as active as the talker. Engage with his message. Allow the words to spark your own ideas. Ask questions as they occur to you. While you need to hear the talker's message, you should also be prepared to lead him to give you the information you need. Ask questions that will produce data relevant to you and to the enterprise.

This is no time to relax. If you truly "need" someone's "advice and counsel," listen in a way that offers the best chance of actually getting it.

**Lesson 29**

## A Lesson Learned

"Yes, when I am going into public places."

~Response to a question about whether he
routinely carried a firearm, 1902

Having assumed the presidency after the assassination of President McKinley, Theodore Roosevelt could have asked for additional Secret Service protection. He did not, but the Secret Service acted on its own and added more guards. The new president took to evading and eluding his bodyguards as a kind of sport.

The truth was that Roosevelt did not trust others to protect his life. He even believed that the beefed-up security detail would interfere with his own efforts to defend himself. He was fatalistic about a stealthy attack from behind. He didn't feel he—or anyone else—could do much about an unseen assailant. However, he expressed confidence that, if a would-be assassin attacked from the front—as had happened in the case of McKinley—he would possess the presence of mind, the strength, the will, and the reflexes to defend himself. All he needed was a good revolver, and so he carried one.

**Some thought TR's** often-expressed faith in his ability to defend himself against an assassin boastful and foolhardy. And so it would have been, had he not armed himself and had he not been comfortably skilled with firearms. You should never boast without possessing the means of making good on what you claim. Take no risk without supplying whatever is required to stack the odds heavily in your favor.

*Lesson 30*
## Have a Hero

"Lincoln is my hero."
~Letter to Sir George Otto Trevelyan, March 9, 1905

"Lincoln is my hero," President Roosevelt wrote to his friend the British historian and statesman George Otto Trevelyan. "He was a man of the people who always felt with and for the people, but who had not the slightest touch of the demagogue in him." The president elaborated, citing Lincoln's "unfaltering resolution, his quiet, unyielding courage, his infinite patience and gentleness, and the heights of disinterestedness which he attained whenever the crisis called for putting aside self." He added praise for Lincoln's "far-sighted, hard-headed common sense" and concluded that, in sum, Lincoln's qualities "point him out as just the kind of chief who can do most good in a democratic republic like ours."

There are two great lessons in this presidential letter.

The first is the precision of Roosevelt's catalogue of Lincoln's qualities. He lists and describes each with great care because they are specific rather than general or vague qualities. They are qualities Roosevelt clearly believed were essential to "do most good in a democratic republic." Look closely at them:

1. *Lincoln was empathetic without descending to demagoguery.*
In his letter to Trevelyan, President Roosevelt was very particular in describing the United States government as a "democratic republic," not simply a democracy. Whereas a democracy is ruled by the will of the people, a democratic republic is governed by leaders who take into account the will of the people, but rather than directly representing it, represent what they judge to be the best interests of the people. This requires empathy combined with clearness of judgment and a refusal to yield leadership just because a majority (or a loud minority) clamors for some particular

action. A demagogue invariably gives the people what they say they want. A leader endeavors to give them what they need.

2. *Lincoln was resolute, quietly and unyieldingly courageous, patient, and gentle.* A fine list of qualities for any leader.

3. *Lincoln could be disinterested and egoless when the situation called for it.* Capable leaders exploit opportunities and fix problems. They do not attempt to exploit or fix people. They do not insist on pitting their ego against the egos of others.

4. *He possessed common sense that was both practical ("hard-headed") and visionary ("far-sighted").* A successful leader was able to join the practical to the visionary without sacrificing one to the other.

The second lesson is this: Theodore Roosevelt had a hero.

He identified an archetype of the leader he wanted to be, he analyzed that archetype, and we can confidently assume that he modeled himself after it. "I think of Lincoln, shambling, homely, with his strong, sad, deeply-furrowed face, all the time," he wrote to an acquaintance. "I see him in the different rooms and in the halls [of the White House]. . . . So far as one who is not a great man can model himself upon one who was, I try to follow out the general lines of policy which Lincoln laid down."

**Study leaders in every** industry, every enterprise, every context, and in every age. Acquire a worthy hero—or two, maybe three, or even more. Emulate the best of them.

*Lesson 31*
## Dig Deep

"Wrestling is simply a sport with rules almost as conventional as those of tennis, while jiu jitsu is really meant for practice in killing or disabling your adversary."

~Letter to his son Kermit, February 24, 1905

While he was in the White House, President Roosevelt not only boxed, a sport with which he was long familiar, but also took up jiu jitsu, an activity most Americans would have found exotic beyond easy understanding. And that is precisely what intrigued him about it.

His letter to his son Kermit hints at the roots of his interest in this martial art. Whereas wrestling was a sport, governed by rules that were ultimately "conventional" and therefore superficial, jiu jitsu was a deadly serious business. It ran deep. Its rules were not conventions, but deadly weapons—and, what is more, they were weapons that exploited an adversary's own strength not merely to defeat him but to disable or to kill him. No combative system could dig deeper than that.

> **Often identified with such** phrases as *avid sportsman*, Theodore Roosevelt was never very satisfied with mere sport. His urge was always to get beneath and beyond the superficiality of convention that ultimately divides sport from life. An idealist, he nevertheless sought always to confront, engage, grapple, and master physical reality. His life offers a two-word lesson to leaders who want to be more than just scorekeepers: *Dig deep.*

■

## *Lesson 32*
## Count Ten

> "What a place the Presidency is for learning to keep one's temper."
>
> ~Letter to his son Kermit, June 17, 1906

Before he entered the White House, Roosevelt had earned a reputation for having a short-fused and highly explosive temper. Once in power as the nation's chief executive, however, he quickly learned that a short temper served neither his country nor himself.

He discovered two secrets to keeping his temper.

First, he needed always to remember that he was the president of everyone, so that he could afford to alienate no one.

Second, he needed always to understand that his job was, first and last, to find solutions to problems and means to exploit opportunities. To the extent that he could perform these tasks by directing himself to the problems and the opportunities rather than to the personalities and egos associated with them, he found himself encountering fewer occasions for angry outbursts.

**Authority and the power** that comes with it will inflate any ego and therefore tempt virtually any leader to give free rein to emotion. Fight the temptation. The higher up you find yourself, the less room you have for the exercise of ill temper. Provoked? Count ten. Suck it up. Put everything into your job.

■

## *Lesson 33*
## Value Adversity

> "The men who have made our national greatness are those who faced danger and overcame it, who met difficulties and surmounted them, not those whose paths were cast in such pleasant places that toil and dread were ever far from them."
>
> ~Speech, Galena, Illinois, April 27, 1900

For Theodore Roosevelt, the great lesson of living was the value of everything in life, including adversity in every form. In his vision, the universe was an intensely moral place in which everything served a purpose, including danger and difficulty. Sources of threat, pain, and failure, these invited conquest by the resolute striver. Without adversity, there could be no greatness—indeed, no real achievement. Without the prospect of failure, there could be no true success.

For Roosevelt, the magnitude of any accomplishment was measured against the degree of difficulty, danger, risk, and adversity. The purpose of life was not to avoid struggle, but to struggle. If the ultimate risk in this scheme was death, so much the better. As TR wrote to his close friend Cecil Spring-Rice on March 12, 1900, "Death is always and under all circumstances a tragedy, for if it is not, then it means that life itself has become one." In the inevitable prospect of death, Theodore Roosevelt found both tragedy and the alternative to tragedy: a life lived to its very extremity and, therefore, its highest possible worth.

**One of the hardest** and most important things a leader must do is to "sell" risk to his stakeholders. Begin by ensuring that you have assessed the risk realistically, then present it realistically, neither exaggerating costs and consequences nor minimizing them. But, above all, acquire the habit of presenting risk not in terms of the negative consequences of failure, but as the ultimate source of value in any achievement. Risk is not merely the cost of reward. It is both the foundation and definition of reward. At the outset of any collective endeavor, define it not as a potential liability but offer it as an actual asset, a necessity joyous rather than grim.

■

# 3

Lead the
Teaching
Life

## Lesson 34
## Fighting Words

> "Don't let anyone impose on you. Don't be quarrelsome, but stand up for your rights. If you've got to fight, fight and fight hard and well."
>
> ~ Christmas talk to schoolchildren at Oyster Bay, New York, 1898

Theodore Roosevelt came of age in a world that saw life as combat, whether in the wild realm of nature or the so-called civilization of humankind. It was a world that had been explained by Darwin ("nature red in tooth and claw," as the poet Alfred, Lord Tennyson put it) and by Darwin's social interpreter Herbert Spencer, who coined the phrase "survival of the fittest" to describe the processes of both natural evolution and social evolution. Far from bemoaning this outlook of combative struggle as grim, Roosevelt found it exhilarating. He was a warrior, and a joyous one at that.

His advice to children in 1898 would doubtless be unwelcome in today's more emotionally fastidious climate. But his words are worth examining closely for what they say about establishing one's place in any organization.

*Don't let anyone impose on you.* Did the children in TR's audience fully understand the word *impose?* More to the point, do we today? Roosevelt was a writer, one who thought carefully about the words he used. At its root, *impose* means to "put upon" or to "force upon." To impose on another is to force something—oneself, one's will, one's demand—on another. Roosevelt had no objection to informed and intelligent compliance, especially for the common good, but he saw in the attempt at imposition an ample reason to fight. To yield your will to outside force was to abandon liberty, democracy, and morality.

*Don't be quarrelsome, but stand up for your rights.* Don't pick fights, Roosevelt advised, but always defend rights. If you don't, you will lose them.

*If you've got to fight, fight and fight hard and well.* The important thing here is that Roosevelt does not speak of winning but of fighting hard and well. *Winning* is an outcome. *Fighting hard and well is a conduct—*an action, an effort. For him, the outcome was always of less consequence than the personal struggle toward that outcome. Each of us, he understood, bears responsibility for what we do, but not necessarily for the results of what we do.

> **You will look in** vain to find *fighting* in the curriculum of any modern management course. Today, we prize "avoiding" conflict and, if unavoidable, "resolving" it as rapidly and as smoothly as possible. TR's nearly two terms in office were periods of peace and plenty, and in 1906 he was awarded the Nobel Peace Prize for his role in negotiating an end to the Russo-Japanese War. Yet no American president has a more bellicose reputation than Teddy Roosevelt. Moreover, it was a reputation he savored.
>
> Brand yourself as Theodore Roosevelt did. Then let no one impose on your brand. Draw the line here, but negotiate everything else. The results matter less than what you say and do in producing them.

■

*Lesson 35*
## Advantage: Optimism

"I am an optimist, but I hope I am a reasonably intelligent one."

~Letter to Owen Wister, February 27, 1895

From early in life, Roosevelt proclaimed himself an optimist and an apostle of optimism. It was an orientation he based on a balanced assessment of the world. As he wrote to Wister, "I recognize that all the time there are numerous evil forces at work, and that in places and at times they outweigh the forces that tend for good," but he judged that "Hitherto, on the whole, the good have come out ahead," and he had faith that "they will in the future."

**Clearly, Roosevelt's optimism** was more considered than arbitrary. Could he have come to another conclusion? Perhaps. But there would have been no productive benefit to it. As an approach to life, pessimism is a brake rather than an engine. Find some credible way to become—to be—and to remain an optimist. It is the only viable option for a leader.

■

*Lesson 36*
## Teach the Hard Lessons

"No matter if you think the law is a bad one; you must see that your men carry out your orders to the letter."
~ Police Board president Roosevelt to his officers, June 10, 1895

New York City's Sunday Excise Law, which banned the sale of alcohol by saloons on Sunday, had been on the books for thirty-eight years when Theodore Roosevelt became president of the Police Board in 1895. Throughout those thirty-eight years, the law had been almost totally unenforced. As the new police commissioner, Roosevelt had nothing in particular against Sunday liquor sales, but he nevertheless resolved to make enforcement of the Sunday Excise Law a top priority of his administration. His purpose was not to keep people from drinking on the Sabbath, but to teach New

Yorkers–civilians as well as police officers–respect for the law, even an unpopular one.

He knew that his campaign of enforcement would draw criticism, but he told reporters, "I do not deal with public sentiment. I deal with the law." The saloon law was unpopular. Maybe it was even a bad law. But it was the *law*. "How I might act as a legislator, or what kind of legislation I should advise, has no bearing on my conduct as an executive officer charged with administering the law," he explained.

When, two years later, Roosevelt stepped down as New York's top cop to accept appointment as President McKinley's assistant secretary of the navy, there were, doubtless, many New Yorkers who cheered his departure. Yet the *New York Times* was representative of the more considered popular opinion, which was one of gratitude for "service . . . rendered to the city [that had been] second to that of none." Of the many reforms he introduced to the NYPD–reforms that lifted it from the status of national scandal to a model police force for the nation's big cities–perhaps the most valuable was a hard and unpopular lesson about the nature of law and the necessity of giving every law the respect it demanded.

**As president of the** New York City Police Board from 1895 to 1897, Theodore Roosevelt understood his duty as an *executive*: literally as the chief administrator charged with *executing* the law as it existed. His job was not to attempt to pass new laws or to revise existing laws. Nevertheless, he decided that, in order to execute the law, he was required to step beyond the role of administrator and become a teacher. He saw that, to administer the law adequately and efficiently, he had to deliver a lesson in respect for the law. It was not an easy or a pleasant or a popular lesson, but it was a necessary lesson, and so he taught it.

As a leader, you are called on to create as well as to administer policy, plans, and programs. Often, the most efficient way to do this is by educating those on whom the success or failure of a policy, plan, or program depends. Teach the members of your organization the lessons they need to build the future of the enterprise. Some are bound to be hard and unpopular lessons. Often, these are the most critically important.

■

*Lesson 37*
## Advice to Children

"There are two things that I want you to make up your minds to: first, that you are going to have a good time as long as you live–I have no use for the sour-faced man–and next, that you are going to do something worthwhile, that you are going to work hard and do the things you set out to do."
~Christmas talk to schoolchildren at Oyster Bay, New York, 1898

When he spoke to the children of Oyster Bay, his hometown, he might just as well have been speaking to himself. His close friend Cecil Spring-Rice observed, "You must always remember that the President is about six." A big part of his advice to children on how to "grow up" was *never* to grow up–or at least, never to forget the best part of childhood in the process of growing up.

The business of a child is to have a good time. Teddy Roosevelt was determined to expand that business into a whole life's work. His best modern biographer, Edmund Morris, described his "irresistible laugh" as "an eruption of mirth, rising gradually to falsetto chuckles, that convulses everybody around him." The laughter was a naturally childlike expression of the perpetually youthful energy of a man having the time of his life. But as with a child engrossed in play, the Roosevelt exuberance was also capable of intense focus. Have fun for the rest of your life, he advised the children, *and* "work hard [to] do the [worthwhile] things you set out to do."

> **The America into which** Theodore Roosevelt was born presented itself as a soberly earnest place, a place that demanded "knuckling down" to "get down to brass tacks" while "keeping your head down" and your "nose to the grindstone." The operative word was *down* and the words surrounding *down* were of hard, unpleasant things: *knuckles, brass,* and *grindstones.* In many ways, Roosevelt was the product of this world—a man with serious moral intentions and high ideals—but what set him apart was the joy he took in all that he did. His work was play, and the vehicle of his leadership was sheer exuberance. Learn to lead your enterprise in work as if it were child's play.

■

*Lesson 38*
## Tell Them Who They Are

"This nation is seated on a continent flanked by two great oceans. It is composed of . . . the descendants of pioneers, or, in a sense, pioneers themselves; of men winnowed out from among the nations of the Old World by the energy, boldness, and love of adventure found in their own eager hearts. Such a nation, so placed, will surely wrest success from fortune."

~Speech from the White House, December 2, 1902

A prolific author and speaker, Theodore Roosevelt was in large measure a teacher, a mentor to the people who had read him, who listened to him, and who elected him. His chief lesson, repeated over and over again and rephrased as the context and occasion required, was one of identity. He was forever telling the American people who they are.

President Roosevelt was a historian of considerable merit and reputation, but, for him, history was not a succession of documented facts. It was instead a grand narrative of meticulously documented mythology. For him—as for many other writers, including historians, of his age—the central mythology in American history was the role of the pioneer in creating a distinctive national identity. President Roosevelt applied that mythology historically, explaining to contemporary Americans how their common pioneer past created a defining legacy, but also insisted that it continued to be produced in the present. The United States of TR's day was very much a nation of immigrants. These newcomers, the president argued, were not literal sons and daughters of the first pioneers, but they were, properly speaking, pioneers themselves, whose decision to come to America was prima facie evidence of "the energy, boldness, and love of adventure . . . in their own eager hearts" that constituted the very essence of the pioneer, whether one, two, or three hundred years ago or today. Thus President Roosevelt endeavored to unite in a single pioneer identity all Americans: those whose ancestors arrived on the *Mayflower* and those who had just emerged from the Great Hall at Ellis Island. The payoff of understanding this common American identity was not only the enhancement of national unity, but an understanding that this unity was special. It placed every American in a nation that existed apart from the rest of the world, yet that continually drew to itself all of the rest of the world. The unity Roosevelt both defined and preached was the source of a destiny of success wrested from mere fortune.

**Over the course of** your career as a manager or an executive, you will be tasked with leading your organization to achieve many objectives toward attaining many goals. The very first place to which you must lead yourself and the other people of your enterprise, however, is a thorough, persuasive, and inspiring knowledge of just who, both individually and collectively, you all are. Give your organization a productive, winning identity.

■

*Lesson 39*
## You Are the Most Potent Instrument of Leadership You Possess

"Example is the most potent of all things."
~ Address to the Holy Name Society, Oyster Bay,
New York, August 16, 1903

A professional writer, Theodore Roosevelt wrote all his own political and official speeches, and he took great pride in them. The fact was, however, that although he was certainly an emphatic and impassioned orator, he never rose to the heights of eloquence that characterize Abraham Lincoln before him or John F. Kennedy after him. Yet no one can deny that he was, far more often than not, a highly effective speaker.

As much as Roosevelt loved to speak, he held one instrument of communication above speechmaking when it came to leading his nation. That instrument was himself. More precisely, it was himself applied as a well-crafted and vivid example to others.

As he saw it, the president was no mere administrator. His highest duty was to be nothing less than a model for national behavior. His professional calling was to shape himself into the ideal American.

It is said that, in ancient societies, the tribal leader or king was a kind of spiritual vessel containing the essence of the tribe or the kingdom. In rhetorical terms, the leader was the *synecdoche* of all that he led. That is, he was a kind of grand metaphor—the part who fully stood for the whole, the representative man. Among modern American leaders, Theodore Roosevelt most closely approached this ancient paradigm. He identified himself as an American, and he expected that the American people would˙ thoroughly identify themselves with him. He offered leadership by example in its most dedicated, intense, even extreme form.

> **"Do as I say, not** as I do" was for Theodore Roosevelt both an absurd and a thoroughly reprehensible leadership dictum. Uncompromising leadership required an uncompromising mode of communication, a mode *beyond* words. What it called for was nothing less than the running total of the life, the decisions, and the deeds of the leader himself. Example is leadership at full potency, utterly unadulterated, unmediated, and undiluted.

■

## *Lesson 40*
## Don't Wallow in Bad News

> "Expose the crime and hunt down the criminal; but remember that, even in the case of crime, if it is attacked in sensational, lurid, and untruthful fashion, the attack may do more damage to the public mind than the crime itself."
>
> ~Speech, Washington, D.C., April 14, 1906

From the start of his political career, Theodore Roosevelt was a reformer. He was elected to his first office, as a New York State assemblyman, at the start of an era of reform, and, beginning with his friendship with New York newspaperman and photographer Jacob Riis—whose *How the Other Half Lives* awakened the nation to the realities of sweatshop and slum life in New York City—he would support a distinguished group of journalists and writers who dedicated themselves to exposing corruption and injustice wherever they found it. Roosevelt even coined the label history has affixed to the likes of Riis, and other reform-minded writers such as Lincoln Steffens (author of *The Shame of the Cities*, 1904, which explored the rampant political corruption in the nation's biggest cities), Ida Tarbell (her 1904 *The History of Standard Oil* detailed the excesses of a great vertical monopoly), and Upton Sinclair (whose 1906 novel *The Jungle* exposed, in detail both lingering and nauseating, the sordid practices of the meatpacking industry). "Muckrakers," the president called them.

It was not a pretty word.

For as much as President Roosevelt admired the crusading reporters and believed them essential to the Progressive movement he himself led, he had also begun to fear that the effects of relentless "muckraking" were themselves corrosive, eroding American idealism even in the very process of the attempt to cleanse America. Muckraking was in danger of becoming indistinguishable from the cheap and lurid sensationalism of "yellow journalism," which the president believed to be a dangerous blight on the era, a practice (he wrote in 1909) that "deifies the cult of the mendacious, the sensational, and the inane," doing "as much to vulgarize and degrade the popular taste, to weaken the popular character, and to dull the edge of the popular conscience, as any influence under which the country can suffer."

Roosevelt's own use of the muckraking image came from *The Pilgrim's Progress*, a Christian allegorical novel by the seventeenth-century British writer John Bunyan, which was a classic most Americans of his day had read at home, in school, or in Sunday school. One of Bunyan's allegorical characters used a "muckrake" to clean up the (moral) filth around him, concentrating so intently on his task that he remained oblivious of the celestial beauty above. Those writers Roosevelt called the "muckrakers" exposed corruption and exploitation rampant in Gilded Age America, attacking child labor practices, slum life, racial persecution, prostitution, sweatshop labor, and the general sins of big business and urban machine politics, but, in so doing (Roosevelt came to believe) provided only a partial version of the truth. They painted a sordid picture of a degenerate nation rather than revealing evils in the broader context of an otherwise great nation.

"The men with the muck rakes are often indispensable to the well-being of society," Roosevelt explained in a speech of April 14, 1906, "but only if they know when to stop raking the muck, and to look upward to the celestial crown above them. . . . If they gradually grow to feel that the whole world is nothing but muck, their power of usefulness is gone."

**Examine your organization,** warts and all, but avoid so magnifying the warts that they become all that you or anyone else can see. Your objective is to improve, elevate, advance, and prosper your enterprise, not to condemn it and leave it wallowing in the muck.

■

*Lesson 41*
## Practice What You Preach

"Of course, the man who preaches decency and straight dealing occupies a peculiarly contemptible position if he does not try himself to practise what he preaches."

~ "Applied Ethics," William Belden Noble Lecture
for 1910, Harvard University

Speaking to the audience of Harvard's venerable William Belden Noble lecture series, Roosevelt made little effort to strike an original note. In counseling his listeners to make it their policy to practice what they preached, he was hardly issuing an original piece of advice. But that doesn't mean it wasn't important to have offered it.

Words were of great importance to Theodore Roosevelt, prolific author and speechmaker, but they ranked below deeds in their power to reveal the true character of a person. The most effective way to get to know someone from the ground up and inside out was to evaluate just how that person's words fit her deeds. The person who preached a policy, and then moved heaven and earth to institute that policy was one formidably persuasive and credible human being.

**It feels good to** forgive, and perhaps for this reason, most people have a generous capacity for forgiveness. Just about everyone, however, draws the line at hypocrisy, and no sin, save actual crime, undercuts a leader's credibility more thoroughly and irreparably than that of preaching one course and taking another. Strive to maintain a perfect harmony between what you say and what you do.

■

*Lesson 42*
## Performance as Public Relations

"No foreign country expected that we could send [the Great White Fleet] around the world in the shape in which we sent it, because none of the foreign countries of the greatest naval power believed that they themselves could do it; and they were proportionately impressed not only by the fact that we did it but by the way in which it was done—by the fact that the fleet, after being away for a year and a quarter, and circumnavigating the globe, came back, having kept to the minute every appointment on its schedule, and reached home in far better fighting trim as regards both men and ships than when it had sailed. That impressed all responsible statesmen abroad much more keenly even than it impressed our own people."

~Speech, Harvard University, December 14, 1910

On December 16, 1907, President Roosevelt sent sixteen battleships of the U.S. Atlantic Fleet on a grand circumnavigation that must stand as one of history's greatest efforts in public relations. The "Great White Fleet" the press and the public called it, because of its peacetime livery of gleaming white adorning the ships' hulls. The president's objective was to proclaim to the world that the United States possessed both the will and the capacity to project its might and influence anywhere on the planet, whether across the Atlantic or the Pacific, which Roosevelt was eager to identify as what he called American "home waters."

By most counts, Theodore Roosevelt published thirty-seven books in his lifetime along with innumerable articles and contributions to the books of others. He was, of course, a prolific speechmaker as well. To stock his writer's mind and imagination he read voraciously. It is believed that he did not let a day go by without reading, start to finish, at least one book. He was, in short, a man who relished language and reveled in it, yet, in the end, the language he found most powerful was a tongue without words. It was action. More specifically, it was the message communicated by a demonstration of performance on a grand scale and at a high level of excellence. This communication in mind, muscle, and steel was the most potent form of public relations and international diplomacy.

**Businesses lavish much** time and money on crafting and communicating their *brand*. It's well that they do so. Branding is very important. But no advertising agency or PR firm can project your brand more forcefully than you and your

> organization can do through actual performance. Your goal
> must always be to impress and to overwhelm. You must strive
> to achieve this goal over and over again.

■

## Lesson 43
## Avoid Sterile Debate

"I have not the slightest sympathy with debating contests in which
each side is arbitrarily assigned a given proposition and told to
maintain it without the least reference to whether those
maintaining it believe in it or not. . . . What we need is to turn out
of our colleges young men with ardent convictions on the side of
right; not young men who can make good arguments for either
right or wrong, as their interest bids them."

~ *An Autobiography*, 1913

Theodore Roosevelt attended Columbia Law School after his
undergraduate years at Harvard, but left without taking a degree. It
was almost certainly just as well. To have argued a case
dispassionately, as a lawyer often must, would have gone directly,
harshly, and destructively against his grain. As he saw it, intellect
without conviction was like strength without intelligence: brutish
and immoral. Talent, ability, and training were worse than useless if
they were unconnected to service in a cause worth believing in and
therefore worthy serving.

He had, in short, no use for arguments conducted for
argument's sake. If you were going to argue a position, you had
better strive to carry the day. Doing so was strenuous, and TR
considered it wrong—criminal, even—to spend your strength in the
service of anything less than the right as you most ardently

understood it. Struggling to grasp what was right, then investing your strength, wit, and learning in its defense—this was the only ethics Theodore Roosevelt accepted. It created in him a passionate exuberance of expression that few could resist.

> **If you acknowledge,** define, understand, and embrace your ardent convictions and allow them to drive your leadership, you will be shocked to discover within yourself depths of persuasion and authority you never have imagined you possessed, let alone so forcefully commanded.

*Lesson 44*
## Avoid Fetish Thinking

"There is superstition in science quite as much as there is superstition in theology, and it is all the more dangerous because those suffering from it are profoundly convinced that they are freeing themselves from all superstition."

~ *The Outlook*, December 2, 1911

Roosevelt was by early attitude and inclination a scientist, who, driven by intense curiosity about nature, formed his conceptions of reality and truth based on observable data. His very first book was a work of scientific observation, *The Summer Birds of the Adirondacks*, published in 1877, when he was not yet nineteen.

He adhered to the scientific habit of mind his whole life. A great believer in enduring principle, he nevertheless weighed everything against the results he observed. The value of truth was fixed and eternal, but the nature of truth was, for him, dynamic, the product of the interaction between a morally informed intelligence and the outside world. To turn your back on this essential dynamism and instead accept as necessarily true any process of understanding or set of beliefs was to make a superstitious fetish of that process and those beliefs, whether you called them "science," "theology," or something else.

For Roosevelt, the still point in his worldview was confidence in his own ability to distinguish between right and wrong, truth and lie, value and worthlessness. It was never an absolute faith in anything outside of himself.

> **Among her many other** roles, a leader is an arbiter, whose evaluations of truth, validity, risk, and value guide the organization. Rely on your perception and judgment. Never surrender them to some fixed system imposed from outside of yourself, no matter what its practitioners call it or what ownership of truth they claim for it. To do so is to trade thinking for fetish thinking, which is a very bad bargain.

■

## *Lesson 45*
## Study to Teach

> "From the standpoint of the nation, and from the broader standpoint of mankind, scholarship is of worth chiefly when it is productive, when the scholar not merely receives or acquires, but gives."
>
> ~ *The Outlook,* January 13, 1912

A man of restless and intense—to use his favorite adjective, "strenuous"—nature, Theodore Roosevelt was also a scholar and writer of scholarly works. His histories, beginning with his 1882 *The Naval War of 1812*, were all intended to teach lessons applicable in the present and to stimulate, aid, and guide preparation for the future. *The Naval War of 1812*, for example, was adopted as a required textbook at the U.S. Naval Academy, largely for the purpose of illustrating the importance of maintaining a strong navy and using it as the basis for formulating a favorable foreign policy. It is no accident that Roosevelt built on the naval scholarship that produced his 1882 history when, as assistant secretary of the navy during the administration of President William McKinley, he championed, engineered, and generally shaped the unprecedented modernization and expansion of the U.S. Navy into a force capable of projecting U.S. diplomacy across two oceans.

Roosevelt valued scholarship, and he relished the company of scholars, but, to him, scholarship was nothing more than self-indulgent dilettantism unless it produced genuinely useful lessons, which were to be valued in proportion to their proving powerful, persuasive, and public. Scholars were to be builders of nations and civilizations. That was their duty, and that was how they were to pull their weight in American society and civilization.

**A leader is a teacher,** who should acquire knowledge voraciously with the purpose of sharing it prodigally. Do not stop with using research to improve the products and services of your own organization. Look for ways to project the influence of your enterprise beyond its four walls, its particular supply chain, and its balance sheet by sharing valuable information with your industry and your community. To enlighten the world is to create a richer marketplace, which will add to everyone's bottom line, including and especially yours.

■

## *Lesson 46*
## Summon Them to a Higher Calling

"We, here in America, hold in our hands the hope of the world, the fate of the coming years; and shame and disgrace will be ours if in our eyes the light of high resolve is dimmed, if we trail in the dust the golden hopes of men."

~Speech, New York City, March 20, 1912

TR thought big, talked big, and acted big. Even the concept of *big*, as he conceived it, was itself big, extending into all dimensions: physical, political, philosophical, moral, spiritual, and ideal. He was by no means the first American president to see the United States as what Abraham Lincoln so movingly described as the "last best hope of earth," but, more than any other of the nation's leaders before or since, he managed to infuse this concept into his public remarks.

His emphasis was always on balancing the awesome power the national mission implied—we "hold in our hands the hope of the world, the fate of the coming years"—with the terrible consequences of failure to accomplish the mission: "shame and disgrace will be ours . . . if we trail in the dust the golden hopes of men." He had put this in even more specific and dramatic terms years earlier, in his 1905 *Inaugural Address*, declaring: "If we fail, the cause of free self-government throughout the world will rock to its foundations."

TR burned to make the United States ever bigger and more powerful. Yet this growth and expansion were to come not at the expense of the world, but for its enrichment. The American mission, as he saw it, was a burden to be willingly accepted. It was to lead and enlighten humankind. As he saw it, to be a world power was to exercise influence not so much over lands as over minds, hearts, and souls. The rewards of this endeavor were without bounds, even as the consequences of faltering and failing were without bottom.

**Responsibility increases with power.** Too many managers and executives make the mistake of attempting to motivate the members of their enterprise by framing the promise of power in terms of the great privileges it will bring. Theodore Roosevelt made no such error. Instead, he framed power in terms of responsibility—what he always called *duty*—and put the emotional emphasis of his public appeals on the consequences of shirking the duty that comes with power. No motive is more sustainable that a keen moral consciousness of the higher stakes of performance and the failure of performance.

■

## Lesson 47
## How to Make History Useful

"History, taught for a directly and immediately useful purpose to pupils and the teachers of pupils, is one of the necessary features of a sound education in democratic citizenship."

~ *History as Literature and Other Essays*, 1913

A graduate of Harvard College, Theodore Roosevelt was a great believer in education. He was especially enthusiastic about the subject of history, and he himself wrote a number of history books, including one, *The Naval History of the War 1812*, that was long used as a textbook at the United States Naval Academy in Annapolis, Maryland.

As a historian, Roosevelt was neither a great writer of narrative (though he was often a very *good* one) nor a historical theoretician. What he sought in the study of history were models and lessons to apply "directly and immediately" to some "useful purpose." For him, the past was a trove of the experience of others, and he was determined to pillage it for every scrap of information he and his readers could use. Properly approached, history was a great book that the historian had merely to transcribe clearly and accurately, ensuring that the most useful "lessons" were always the most brilliantly highlighted.

**Too many business** leaders shun the past in a determination to be seen as resolutely forward looking. The experience as well as the work of predecessors is often discarded as the "new boss" endeavors to make his own distinctive mark. The impulse to clean house and to wipe the slate is a powerful one. But to arbitrarily discard history is to violate Roosevelt's gospel of conservation. Approached not with reverence on the one hand or scholarly detachment on the other, but, rather, as a source of directly useful ideas, the past is a commodity far too precious and valuable to be squandered.

■

*Lesson 48*
## Shun the Unmeaning

"One of our defects as a nation is a tendency to use what have been called 'weasel words.' When a weasel sucks an egg the meat is sucked out of the egg; and if you use a 'weasel word' after another there is nothing left of the other."

~Speech, St. Louis, May 31, 1916

As much as he cherished words, Theodore Roosevelt could not bring himself to put his final trust in them. He remarked in a letter to Owen Wister on July 7, 1915, that he had "a perfect horror of words that are not backed up by deeds." For the problem with words is that they could be rendered so slippery as to become almost totally unmeaning. This dissolution of sense was, he believed, becoming a national malady among many in public life. It was a contagion spread by "a tendency to use what have been called 'weasel words.'" These were especially insidious expressions that sounded as if they had meaning, and as if they carried truth, yet they had actually been sucked dry of sense, much as a weasel was said to suck the yolk and white from an egg, leaving only the hollow shell—the appearance of content without the content itself.

Weasel words include vague expressions (references to "some people," "many people," "top experts"), euphemisms and circumlocutions (the straightforward admission "I lied" rendered instead as "my statement is no longer operative"), and passive constructions that remove all responsibility ("I made mistakes" expressed as "mistakes were made"). The great danger, as Roosevelt pointed out, was that weasel words were not only in themselves ultimately meaningless, but they tended to render everything that followed them meaningless as well. They created verbiage that seemed to communicate but actually conveyed nothing. They were to genuine meaning what counterfeit bills are to genuine currency.

Roosevelt used language to convey truth of fact and feeling. Weasel words had the effect of withholding both fact and feeling. They carried the form of communication without the substance and were, for that reason, appalling to him.

**A committed leader** uses language to reveal, not to conceal or evade meaning. Discipline yourself to avoid weasel words by expressing yourself with precision, connecting things and actions to words by favoring nouns and verbs over adjectives and adverbs, attributing statements of fact and interpretation to specific sources, shunning the passive voice by assigning responsibility for actions and policies ("I decided" rather than "It was decided"), and, above all, simply telling the truth even when you really don't want to.

*Lesson 49*
## You Are the Source

> "A stream cannot rise higher than its source."
> ~Favorite TR saying quoted in Owen Wister,
> *Roosevelt: The Story of a Friendship*, 1930

Roosevelt thought hard and thought frequently about the nature of leadership, explaining to his friend the novelist Owen Wister that "the people can do nothing unless they have a man to get behind." His belief was that the true leader understood he was the source of everything the group, whether a company or a nation, undertook, achieved, became, or would become. Thus it behooved a leader to make himself big. "There is a tendency to believe that a hundred small men can furnish leadership equal to that of one big man," he wrote in the May 1917 issue of the *Ladies' Home Journal.* "This is not so."

So, as he saw it, it behooved Theodore Roosevelt to set himself high, to a place of lofty ideals and visionary ambitions, since no stream can rise higher than its source.

**A leader can enable** or can limit her enterprise. The surest way to avoid the latter is to habitually set goals higher than you think achievable. This done, support unconditionally all efforts to achieve them. You will be amazed at how often the people of your organization will exceed your expectations.

■

*Lesson 50*
## How to Inspire

> "By his words and deeds he gave a defining and supporting frame
> for the aspirations of those insufficiently clear or strong to support

their aspirations by their own endeavor. Men, in the hope of finding their better selves, attached themselves to him."

~Elting E. Morison, Editor's Preface to
*The Letters of Theodore Roosevelt*, 1951–54

Not even his critics deny that Theodore Roosevelt was an "inspiring leader." Unfortunately, however, few phrases are less instructive than "inspiring leader." Beethoven was a "musical genius." Roosevelt was an "inspiring leader." True and true, but what in these labels is there for us to emulate? Be a genius. Be inspiring. Such advice is of no help to anybody.

That is why the comment of Harvard educator, historian, and military biographer Elting E. Morison, the scholar who edited Roosevelt's letters, is so insightful. Brief though the comment is, it provides an analysis of what it actually meant to be an "inspiring leader," at least in the instance of Theodore Roosevelt. Here is what Elting tells us:

1. Roosevelt used language—a "language" made up of words as well as deeds—to define the aspirations of the many who felt some inward aspiration but could not define it.

2. Roosevelt's definition constituted a "frame" to support the endeavors of those others, whose undefined aspirations were "insufficiently clear" to provide the needed support.

3. Because Roosevelt was able to provide definition and support to the undefined and unsupported aspirations of others, he enabled his fellow Americans to embark on a quest for "their better selves."

4. Roosevelt's commitment to American aspirations in turn bound America to him.

**Inspiration is not about** possessing an innately charismatic personality, and it is not a matter of finding or formulating a few magically eloquent words. Instead, it is the business of identifying your own aspirations with those of your enterprise and using that identification to define and to reinforce the ennobling, empowering, and enabling feelings and ideas latent and unexpressed in the members of your organization.

To *inspire* is to breathe life into others. These are the verbs by which this may be accomplished: *empathize, define, encourage, celebrate, share.* These are the nouns on which those verbs must operate to do it: *ideas, dreams, goals— aspirations.*

■

# Lead the
# Innovative
# Life

## Lesson 51
## Justice and "Practicability"

> "In advocating any measure we must consider not only its justice but its practicability."
>
> ~Roosevelt's senior thesis, Harvard College, 1880

In his Harvard senior thesis, Theodore Roosevelt tackled the controversial subject of women's rights in his characteristically innovative manner. Instead of embarking on the well-traveled route of arguing for or against the equality of women, he took the innovative shortcut of defining justice strictly in terms of law:

> "A cripple or a consumptive in the eye of the law is equal to the strongest athlete or the deepest thinker," he wrote, "and the same justice should be shown to a woman whether she is or is not the equal of a man."

The implied parallel with cripples and consumptives suggests that young Roosevelt did not, in fact, think women were the equal of men. In practical terms, however, this sentiment counted for nothing in his argument, since, *under the law*, cripples, consumptives, *and* women were equal to the strongest male athlete and deepest male thinker.

In ideological terms, young Roosevelt hardly showed himself to be a feminist, but his practical definition of equality as defined by law led him to conclusions that might have issued from the pen of the most radical of champions of women's rights. "As regards the laws relating to marriage," he wrote, "there should be the most absolute equality preserved between the two sexes. I do not think the woman should assume the man's name. . . . I would have the word 'obey' used not more by the wife than the husband."

Even this early in his thinking life, Theodore Roosevelt embraced an innovative concept of justice not as a remote ideal but as a "practicable" reality within immediate reach. The justice of treating women as the equals of men was to be found neither in fact nor in ideal nor in theory, but in law. Insofar as the law demanded equality, women were legally the equal of men. As Roosevelt saw it in 1880, this was the only practicable way in which such equality could exist. If one tried to force the definition of justice beyond the boundaries of law, it might well be that a woman is no more the equal of a man than a "cripple" is the equal of the "strongest athlete."

> **As abstract principles,** fairness and justice are of little use to the leader of any organization. Your decisions and actions have no chance of being accepted as objective and equitable unless they have a fair and just effect in the real world. Devise the means of ensuring that your administration of fairness and justice is "practicable," that it does not consist of aspirations, but of decisions and judgments actually and immediately capable of being put into practice.

■

## Lesson 52
### Originate

"It is always better to be an original than an imitation."
~ Comment in *Forum,* April 1894

Theodore Roosevelt came of age in an era of aphorisms. Politicians, statesmen, teachers, pastors, and parents, all were expected in turn-of-the-century America to transmit *words to live by.* In such a moral, philosophical, and literary climate TR's sensibilities as a communicator developed, and, for that reason, much of what he uttered or wrote for public consumption was self-consciously epigrammatic, even expressly intended for quotation. Not all of it strikes a modern reader as worthy of quotation, however, and it becomes all too easy to dismiss some declarations as high-flown statements of the blandly self-evident.

Case in point: "*It is always better to be an original than an imitation.*"

Who could argue with this? Who indeed? Except, perhaps, to question why Theodore Roosevelt took the trouble to write such a self-evident proposition in the first place. Yet he *did* take the trouble to write it, and if we take the trouble to read and reread it, its meaning comes to seem less obvious and more revelatory, especially in light of Roosevelt's own example.

Roosevelt might have written *it is always better to be original than to imitate*, but he did not. He took care to use the word original not as an adjective, but as a noun—a description of the person, not the behavior. Put this way, the proposition becomes not just challenging, but downright daunting. It can be difficult enough to "*be* original," but just how do you go about being "an original"? Must you be born *an* original? Or can you learn to be one? And if you can, wouldn't such learning make you, ipso facto, *an imitation?*

There is no *easy* answer. TR, however, fashioned his entire life into one long and richly complex answer. Just as he chose to use *original* as a noun rather than an adjective, so he defined, by the very conduct of his life, being *an* original in terms of action. He rooted the noun firmly in a verb. What, then, is *an* original? One who *originates*.

From an early age, Roosevelt saw his vocation as leader. A leader is to a follower what an original is to an imitation. A leader originates. A follower imitates. The greatest leader, Roosevelt believed, was the source—the originator—of everything the enterprise required. He was an intellectual, moral, and physical example to all, the pattern for everything.

> **Embrace the proposition** that all your enterprise is and will be, all that it does and will do, originates with you. To be a leader is to be an original.

■

*Lesson 53*
## Be an Innovative Organization Man

"The one thing abhorrent to the powers above the earth and under them is the hyphenated American–the "German-American," the "Irish-American," or the "native-American." Be Americans–pure and simple!"

~Speech, Buffalo, New York, September 10, 1895

In 1956, during the height of what many considered the blissful complacency of the Eisenhower administration, *Fortune* magazine editor William H. Whyte wrote *The Organization Man*, a study of what he saw as a shift in America from individual initiative to total identification with one's corporate employer, which prompted the individual to submerge his self-identity within the collective identity of the organization. Whyte was profoundly disturbed by the emergence of this new "organization man," and the phrase has had an inescapably negative connotation since Whyte used it.

Although Whyte used the phrase and gave it widespread currency, he had not coined it. For many years before his book appeared, big business had been lauding–not condemning–its best, most loyal, and most effective employees as "organization men": the people who enthusiastically identified their success with the success of the enterprise that employed them.

Theodore Roosevelt, who took every possible occasion to celebrate individual initiative, freely urged all Americans to become organization men by identifying themselves wholeheartedly with the nation. His advice to leave the heritage of the "old country" at home, to drop the hyphenated hybrid identity of Irish-American, German-American, Polish-American, even Native-American in favor of, simply, American was (and remains) controversial. He didn't care. He was willing to sacrifice some degree of individual identity for the sake of national cohesion. By no means did branding yourself an "American" require thinking and acting in lockstep with other "Americans." What it did require was thinking and acting in ways designed to benefit the nation, the common enterprise, and not just yourself.

> **"If everybody is thinking** the same way, nobody is thinking," General George S. Patton Jr. liked to say. Theodore Roosevelt would have smiled his trademark toothy grin in agreement, but he would have added—*as long as everybody's thinking about the good of the organization.* Tolerate no hyphenated loyalties. Require total commitment to the enterprise while acknowledging that there are many individual ways to build and to express that commitment. Common goals do not require the end of innovation.

■

*Lesson 54*
## Energize What's Right

> "The corrupt men have been perfectly content to let their opponents monopolize all the virtue while they themselves have been permitted to monopolize all the efficiency."
> ~ *The Outlook*, December 21, 1895

While Theodore Roosevelt was president of the New York City Police Board, he wrote an article explaining the "progressive" innovations of reform he had so dramatically introduced. These had nothing to do with defining the differences between right and wrong. Right and wrong were hardly innovative concepts. Nor did Commissioner Roosevelt innovate new rules. There were plenty of reasonable laws and regulations already on the books. What he *did* introduce was an unprecedented degree of vigilance, vigor, and zeal in the enforcement of the laws, rules, and regulations that were intended to uphold right and suppress wrong. For the first time in a city government long inured to corruption as the status quo, Roosevelt administered virtue with the same energetic efficiency that the "corrupt men" had been applying to the execution of their misdeeds. Right, like wrong, is nothing more than a concept until it is given shape and force by decision and action.

> **Ethics is a potential policy** of business up to the moment that it is rendered *kinetic* by application to every decision you make and every initiative you implement for your organization. If you want an ethical business, energize what's right. Apply ethics efficiently.

■

*Lesson 55*
## Make Proactive Choices

> "Any officer whose instinct was to stoke up before a crisis . . .
> could be trusted in wartime."
> ~Edmund Morris, on Roosevelt's assessment of Commodore George
> Dewey, *The Rise of Theodore Roosevelt,* 1979

Appointed assistant secretary of the navy in 1897, Theodore Roosevelt was by virtue of his job description subordinate to the secretary of the navy. Yet Navy Secretary John D. Long was quick to appreciate his assistant's intellect, competence, and limitless vigor, so consequently gave him a very long leash. It was Roosevelt, the "assistant," who assumed much of the responsibility for preparing the navy to fight what would become the Spanish-American War.

Roosevelt pored over the lists of senior naval officers and encountered one, Commodore George Dewey, who, he noted, had responded to an incipient crisis in Chile back in 1891 by digging into his own pocket to buy coal for the ship he commanded rather than await official orders from navy brass. This proactive instinct so impressed the assistant secretary that he immediately prevailed on Long to ensure that Dewey would be jumped over some more senior officers to be given a top fleet command before the war with Spain broke out.

> **Proactive leadership requires** innovative solutions. Anticipate the need, and then invent your response *before* the response is needed. You will never have more time for innovation than in a period before a crisis hits or an opportunity presents itself.

■

*Lesson 56*
## Don't Stand under a Corpse

Ansley Wilcox: "Don't you think it would be far better to do as the Cabinet has decided?"

Roosevelt: "No. It would be far worse."
~Conversation, September 14, 1901

When word reached Vice President Roosevelt that President William McKinley had succumbed to the wounds inflicted by an assassin days earlier, he descended from remote Mount Marcy, New York, where he had been vacationing, and took a train across the state to Buffalo. He was greeted at the railroad station by longtime friend and Buffalo resident Ansley Wilcox, who invited him to his home at 641 Delaware Avenue for lunch before moving on to the Milburn House, where McKinley's body lay.

During lunch, discussion turned to the subject of where Roosevelt would be sworn in. The vice president cut the discussion short with a single word: "Here."

Wilcox responded that the cabinet had already decided that the ceremony should be held at the Milburn House, in a room directly below that in which McKinley's body lay. When Wilcox posed the rhetorically phrased question, "Don't you think it would be far better to do as the cabinet has decided?" his guest replied flatly: "No. It would be far worse."

Two points leap out in this exchange.

The first is the simple fact that Roosevelt took charge, rejecting the advice of a cabinet his predecessor had appointed and asserting his own decisive will instead.

The second point demonstrates that this assertion of will was not a matter of mere willfulness. Roosevelt had a very good reason for moving the ceremony. He did not say what it was, but we can easily guess it. To him, it seemed a very bad idea to swear in a new president literally beneath the corpse of the old one. It was, to begin with, unseemly, even morbid. On a more precisely symbolic level, such a swearing in seemed to place the new president in the grip of the dead hand of his predecessor. Continuity, Roosevelt understood, was important after the national shock of assassination, but a leader could not lead if he permitted himself to be cast in the shadow of a corpse. Needless to say, the ceremony was held where Roosevelt wanted it.

**Claim your leadership space.** This does not necessarily require radical reinvention. In most cases of succession from one leader to the next, it is useful to maintain a feeling of continuity within the organization. This feeling, however, must not be allowed to limit your range for useful innovation. Create assurances that you will not introduce change for the sake of change, but neither will you feel an obligation to entomb the enterprise in the dead past.

When you step up, move forward. History can guide you, but, first thing, move out of the shadow of the corpse.

■

## *Lesson 57*
## To Think? To Act? To Innovate

"Mr. Roosevelt has taken the whole thing into his own hands, and is keeping it there in the quietest and most unobtrusive manner. He has done a very big and an entirely new thing."

~The *Times* of London, quoted in the *New York Times*,
October 17, 1902

President Roosevelt's deft intervention in the coal strike of 1902 (see Lesson 123, "Protect *Your* Flock"), which averted a potentially deadly wintertime "coal famine" by mediating a workable compromise between miners and mine owners, was widely praised. Not everyone, however, was pleased. George Baer, president of the coal-hauling Philadelphia and Reading Railroad, condemned Roosevelt for having set a socialist precedent by his intervention in the mechanics of the free market. Baer demanded of novelist Owen Wister, the president's longtime intimate, "Does your friend ever think?"

Wister paused before responding quietly: "He certainly seems to act."

What, in fact, Theodore Roosevelt had done in successfully stepping into the apparently insoluble and potentially cataclysmic coal strike was both to think *and* to act in order to innovate. For he had reached the conclusion that the old ways of thinking and acting about the chief executive's role in the relations between capital and labor were tragically inadequate to deal with this case. A "very big and entirely new thing," the *Times* called the president's mediation efforts. "We are witnessing not merely the ending of the coal strike, but the definite entry of a powerful government into a novel sphere of operation."

Into a time-honored system that pitted owners against workers, Theodore Roosevelt had sided with neither, but had instead dared to introduce and uphold the interests of a third party: the people.

> **Pulled by some to think** and pressed by others *to act*, choose your own course. Innovate.

■

*Lesson 58*
## Never Patch What You Need to Replace

> J. P. Morgan: "If we have done anything wrong, send your man to my man and they can fix it up."
>
> Roosevelt: "That can't be done."
> ~Meeting among J. P. Morgan, Attorney General Philander Knox,
> and President Theodore Roosevelt, February 22, 1902

Early in 1902, railroad magnates Edward H. Harriman and James J. Hill and oil mogul John D. Rockefeller joined forces with financier John Pierpont Morgan to create the Northern Securities Company, a giant "trust" (as commercial monopolies were then called) designed to control and combine the Northern Pacific Railway, Great Northern Railway, Burlington Railroad, and other smaller lines. Theodore Roosevelt decided that such a non-competitive monopoly was clearly detrimental to the public interest and directed his attorney general, Philander Knox, to bring suit against Northern Securities under the practically dormant Sherman Antitrust Act of 1890.

Roosevelt intended not merely to win the case, but, in so doing, to create a precedent that would bar the formation of trusts in the future and bring about the dissolution of existing trusts, which he believed were oligarchic, unfair to consumers, unfair to labor, and generally incompatible with the principles of democratic capitalism. When J. P. Morgan met with the president and the attorney general in February 1902, he was genuinely shocked when the president brushed aside his offer to "fix . . . up" whatever was "wrong."

Morgan asked Roosevelt why he was not given the opportunity to correct any "irregularities" in the charter of Northern Securities.

"That is just what we did not want to do," the president explained.

Knox elaborated: "We don't want to fix it up, we want to stop it."

Later, in private, Roosevelt remarked to Knox that Morgan simply didn't get it. The financier could not see that the trust he had created was alien to a democratic society and was, in fact, illegal. Instead, Roosevelt observed, Morgan thought of the president of the United States as nothing more than "a big rival operator" with whom he could strike a deal. If Roosevelt had been in the least tempted to bargain, he did not let on. Almost certainly, he and Knox were speaking the absolute truth when they disavowed any intention of "fixing" Northern Securities. The president had a much larger victory to win, and stopping Northern Securities dead was the only means of winning it.

**Business, like politics,** is rightly said to be the art of compromise. Yet there are some goals and objectives that are killed by compromise. If a proposal, an idea, a program, or a system requires replacement, do not settle for patching it. Make the big changes you really need to make, not just the small changes that are easy and convenient or that you can "get by" with. Compromise where you can. Stand firm where you must.

## Lesson 59
## No Substitute for the Human Machine

"If you put the best of weapons in the hands of a coward, he will be beaten by the brave man with a club."
~ Speech, Kansas City, Missouri, May 1, 1903

Theodore Roosevelt was president at the dawn of what historians would come to call "the American century," a century destined to be dominated by American influence in every dimension, but in none so compellingly as technology.

TR heartily approved. Yet even as he cheered on the American industrial juggernaut, he believed that in any meaningful endeavor, the power of the mere machine was as nothing compared to the force of the human machine. Technology, no matter how potent, was worthless unless it was in the control of a courageous human intelligence. The "contest between man and machine" was a familiar theme in Roosevelt's America. As for the president himself, he regarded that "contest" as no contest at all. Humanity was destined to be the inevitable winner in any race worth the running.

**Give your enterprise the** best weapons technology offers. They are important. They are also absolutely limited by the level of the people into whose hands you put them.

■

## Lesson 60
## Dream and Do

"Keep your eyes on the stars, but remember to keep your feet on the ground."
~ Speech, the Groton School, Groton, Massachusetts, May 24, 1904

One of the most persistent fallacies that cling to the topic of leadership is the belief that vision and idealism are somehow incompatible with practical action. TR confronted this false dichotomy by compulsively *doing* things even as he spun out his *vision* of domestic reform and international dominion for America. His advice to the students of Groton was to dream great dreams while also remaining rooted in practical reality. Impossible? Writers, artists, and musicians do it every day, building a vision from grounding in a thorough knowledge of words and meanings, of paints and pigments, of tones, timbres, and rhythms. Architects build dreams grounded in their knowledge of physics, materials, and structural engineering. Scientists imagine the unimaginable founded on nature observed and the laws of mathematics. In fact, Roosevelt argued, the only path to greatness runs from the ground and up through the stars. "It is true of the Nation," he told an audience in Worcester, Massachusetts, in 1905, "as of the individual, that the greatest doer must also be a great dreamer."

**Everything that was not** here before humanity appeared on the planet began as a thought, a vision, a dream. Although they are without physical substance, these are the genesis of all that is solid and productive.

■

*Lesson 61*
## The Value of an Ideal Must Be Real

"If you have an ideal only good while you sit at home, an ideal that nobody can live up to in outside life, examine it closely, and then cast it away."

~Speech, the Groton School, Groton, Massachusetts, May 24, 1904

"A man is worthless unless he has in him a lofty devotion to an ideal," Roosevelt wrote in *The Outlook* for July 28, 1900, "and he is worthless also unless he strives to realize this ideal by practical methods." Four years later, he expressed this idea more vividly and provocatively to the students of the Groton School. He did not call on them to discard idealism, but to test their ideals in the real world. As a solo act, idealism is without value. The worth of an ideal must be proved on the open stage of outward action, in public, and for the public good.

> **First, commit to idealism.** Second, commit to infusing idealism with reality and reality with idealism. Begin with the group, department, organization, or business you lead.

■

*Lesson 62*
## Find the Inspiration to Innovate

"I have been a little puzzled over the Nobel Prize."
~Letter to his son Kermit, December 5, 1906

Beginning early in 1904, the rival empires of Russia and Japan clashed over expansion into Manchuria and Korea. The rest of the world was stunned by the violence of a war in which some 130,000 military combatants, in addition to perhaps 20,000 Chinese civilians, died as a direct result of battle. Many thousands more succumbed to disease and famine conditions caused by the fighting.

President Roosevelt was not content to sit idly by while the nations slaughtered one another. In the summer of 1905, he successfully prevailed upon both sides in the Russo-Japanese War to meet in the quiet American town of Portsmouth, New Hampshire, and undertake peace talks. Thanks to the president's mediation, the talks, which began on August 5, 1905, concluded just a month later with the signing of the Treaty of Portsmouth that ended the brutal war. The following year, the Nobel committee awarded the American president the 1906 Nobel Peace Prize.

When he received word of the award, Roosevelt wrote to his son Kermit that he was "a little puzzled" over how to respond to it because of the "large sum of money–they say about $40,000.00– that goes with it." He told Kermit that he did not want to "do anything that means the refusal of money which would ultimately come to you children," but he had arrived at the decision that while he was president, he "could not accept money given to me for making peace between two nations, especially when I was able to make peace simply because I was President." He continued: "To receive money for making peace would . . . be a little too much like being given money for rescuing a man from drowning, or for performing a daring feat in war."

Roosevelt continued to ponder the "puzzle" until the nature of the award inspired him to think outside of the box. He innovated a solution by which he *could* accept the money without sacrificing ethics.

On December 10, 1906, he cabled the Norwegian minister for foreign affairs, who was also chairman of the Nobel Committee of the Norwegian Parliament. Noting that "what I did I was able to accomplish only as the representative of the Nation of which, for the time being, I am President," he explained that, "After much thought, I have concluded that the best and most fitting way to apply the amount of the prize is by using it as a foundation to establish at Washington a permanent Industrial Peace Committee." Roosevelt's innovation was in the analogy he drew between the original purpose of the Nobel Peace Prize–to promote peace between nations–and his own proposed objective of promoting "better and more equitable relations among my countrymen who are engaged, whether as capitalists or wage workers, in industrial and agricultural pursuits." He was convinced that this would "carry out the purpose of the founder of the prize; for in modern life it is as important to work for the cause of just and righteous peace in the industrial world as in the world of nations."

> **Opportunity is precious.** Never give up on finding ways to exploit it, even if you have to invent them.

■

*Lesson 63*
## Work with Everything You Have

"I keep my good health by having a very bad temper, kept under good control."
~ Overheard remark to a friend, about 1917, quoted in Hermann Hagedorn, *The Roosevelt Family of Sagamore Hill,* 1954

Theodore Roosevelt was a passionate figure who often seemed barely able to contain himself. He often bathed nude in Washington's Rock Creek Park—in mid winter. He was not infrequently seen swinging himself from tree branches on the White House grounds. (It was his idea of outdoor calisthenics.) He sparred with a professional boxer inside the White House, and when this became insufficiently amusing, he hired a jiu jitsu master to teach him that martial art.

The source of all his energy and ebullience may well have been a perpetually bad temper. And those who knew him best did believe that he was always spoiling for a good fight. Roosevelt himself described his "very bad temper" as something he certainly possessed, but also "kept under good control." He did know himself thoroughly, and he clearly understood that if he let his temper rule him, he would achieve nothing. Instead, Roosevelt seems to have harnessed the fight within him and used it as a steam locomotive uses coal, water, and fire. He let his controlled temper drive him.

You cannot decide what traits, tendencies, and talents you'll be born with, but you can follow the example of Teddy Roosevelt and make the most of whatever you have. Examine who you are. Then innovate and invent to make productive use of it.

■

*Lesson 64*
## Sell What Your Customer Understands

"National efficiency . . . is . . . conservation widely applied."
~ "The New Nationalism," speech at Osawatomie, Kansas,
August 31, 1910

Then as now, conservation—what we today call "environmentalism" or "green living"—could be a hard sell. In early twentieth-century America, conservation was conceptually unfamiliar to most people, and it seemed remote from their needs and wants. Roosevelt "sold" the conservation concept in many ways, including, for a rural Kansas audience in 1910, presenting it as the equivalent of efficiency, a concept not only widely understood, but almost universally admired in industrial America and therefore regarded as a good and profitable thing.

Roosevelt explained conserving natural resources as a policy of ultimate efficiency. Waste, he argued, is incompatible with efficiency. Conservation is the avoidance of waste. Therefore, conservation is the key ingredient in any scheme purporting to be efficient.

If Roosevelt was a visionary—and he most certainly was—he was also a skilled politician who possessed a gift for communicating his vision to others, not only in terms they understood, but in terms they wanted to possess for themselves. Instead of attempting to force-feed the unfamiliar to the uninterested, TR translated his brand-new wares into the familiar and the desirable in an appeal not to altruism but to common sense and self-interest.

**Promote your vision** as you would promote merchandise. Do not sell the *features* inherent in it—the aspects of the vision that appeal to you—but instead sell the *benefits*, which is what those features will confer on anyone who buys your vision. Through compelling language, find ways to render the unfamiliar familiar, to make what is yours theirs.

# Lead the
# Executive
# Life

## *Lesson 65*
## Make a Memorable Entrance

> "Suddenly our eyes . . . became glued on a young man who was coming in through the door."
> ~New York State assemblyman John Walsh, recalling Roosevelt's entrance into the assembly chamber, 1882

Roosevelt biographer Edmund Morris detected a common theme among the recollections of those who witnessed newly elected state assemblyman Theodore Roosevelt enter the capitol at Albany for the first time. It was the "image of a young man bursting through a door and pausing for an instant while all eyes were upon him—an actor's trick that quickly became habitual." And like an actor, young Roosevelt was very particular about his costume. "He wore a single eye-glass," Assemblyman Walsh wrote, "with a gold chain over his ear. He had on a cutaway coat with one button at the top, and the ends of its tails almost reached the tops of his shoes. He carried a gold-headed cane in one hand, a silk hat in the other, and he walked in the bent-over fashion that was the style with the young men of the day."

**Skilled actors and capable leaders** (those most often described as "born leaders") have at least one thing in common. They know how to make a memorable entrance. They get noticed. They materialize in a room as a commanding presence. They take control of the stage.

The ability to burst through the door and draw all eyes to you is a great asset, yet also a great responsibility. If you can take the floor, you will have a splendid platform from which to be heard. This is a wonderful thing—provided you are prepared with something genuinely important to say.

■

### Lesson 66
## Seize the High Ground

"... in bolted Teddy ... as if ejected from a catapult."
~Entry from the diary of New York State assemblyman Isaac Hunt,
quoted in Edmund Morris, *The Rise of Theodore Roosevelt,* 1979

Newly elected assemblyman Theodore Roosevelt entered his first Republican caucus not as a timid neophyte among rough-and-ready political veterans, but with the energy of a boulder lofted by a catapult at a castle under siege. Having stormed the room, Roosevelt did not break his stride but made directly for a position squarely in front of the chairman—the most conspicuous place in the room—and sat himself down, elegantly arrayed in a bespoke suit of stylish evening clothes.

Hunt recorded in his diary how everyone "almost shouted with laughter" to behold such an ostentatious specimen of a "New York dude." Yet when Roosevelt rose to speak, Hunt continued, "our attention was drawn upon what he had to say because there was a force in his remarks."

**Never minimize the impact** of original style. It will likely draw a crowd. Just be aware that your audience expects you to deliver substance commensurate with the importance announced by the container. If it proves to be empty, the crowd will respond to a swindle, and you can be sure it won't be pretty.

*Lesson 67*
## Outrun Worry

"Black care rarely sits behind a rider whose pace is fast enough."

~ *Ranch Life and the Hunting-trail,* 1899

Theodore Roosevelt was hardly immune to depression, anxiety, and worry. The death of his first wife, Alice Hathaway Lee on February 14, 1884, two days after giving birth to daughter Alice and on the very day that Roosevelt's mother died, prompted him to inscribe a bold, black X in his diary, under which he wrote, "The light has gone out of my life."

Over time, Roosevelt recovered, aided in no small measure by the intensity with which he took up the work of his day. Ride hard and fast enough, he believed, and you would leave "black care" in the dust behind you. This principle, which he applied to his personal despair, he also applied to nagging worry about decisions of government. He thought long and hard before he acted, but once he reached his decision, he spurred the horses of execution into a full and unrelenting gallop. He did not brood over a decision made. He implemented it.

**Make it a practice to** sever clearly and irreversibly the execution of a decision from the process by which the decision was reached. You should expect that deciding any issue of consequence will involve difficulty and perhaps even some agony and uncertainty. Allow for much discussion, debate, changes of mind, and reversals of opinion.

The motion of the decision phase quite properly resembles that of a pendulum, swinging back and forth, but the movement of execution must be forward only, with nothing permitted to sap the kinetic energy of momentum. What people call *decisiveness* is really *efficiency of execution.*

**Lesson 68**

## Judge Behavior, Not Personalities

"Avoid the base hypocrisy of condemning in one man what you pass over in silence when committed by another."

~Speech, Cambridge, Massachusetts, March 11, 1890

Teddy Roosevelt made no secret of the kind of people he admired. He liked people with big personalities, open-hearted and vigorous in their approach to life. He liked men and women who thought wisely, observed carefully, and spoke interestingly. By all accounts, Roosevelt was a charming companion and a very warm friend to those—and there were many—whom he befriended. He was, in a word, gregarious.

Yet when it came to taking the lead, he did his best to avoid shaping his attitudes and actions according to personal affinity, affection, or the absence of either. He endeavored to purge personality from his decisions. Instead, he judged behavior—the manifestation of principles through actions—rather than personalities. In this way, he avoided the "base hypocrisy" of favoritism and even the appearance of cronyism. At the risk, perhaps, of appearing cold, he ensured that he would always be seen as fair.

**Discipline yourself to judge** behavior rather than personality. Evaluate results rather than motives. Divorce both friendship and enmity from your efforts to honestly weigh outcomes and accurately assess consequences.

■

**Lesson 69**
## Choose to Live in the Best of Times

> "At no period of the world's history has life been so full of interest
> and of possibilities of excitement and enjoyment."
> ~ "National Life and Character," *Sewanee Review II* (1893–94).

*National Life and Character: A Forecast*, by the British historian Charles H. Pearson, was published in 1894. Its genteel but pervasive message of pessimism prompted from Theodore Roosevelt a measured and thorough ten-thousand-word response, which was published in the *Sewanee Review*. His argument against Pearson's point of view was not that the modern world was overwhelmingly a world of goodness. By no means did Roosevelt close his eyes to the many problems of the age. On the contrary, he opened them wide, but then wrote of "the fearful joy" these problems offered by the very fact that they demanded to be solved.

His conclusion that no period of history has offered a "life . . . so full of interest, and of possibilities of excitement and enjoyment" ultimately said less about the era than about his own resolution with respect to living in the era. He presented no proof, in the manner of the pathologically optimistic Pangloss of Voltaire's *Candide*, that ours was "the best of all possible worlds," but instead presented his choice to live in this world as if it were the best of all possible worlds. The interest, the excitement, the enjoyment—these were products not of a particular time and place, but of a mind and heart belonging to a man who chose to be very much alive in *this* particular time and place.

**The difference between** Charles H. Pearson, author of *National Life and Character*, and Theodore Roosevelt, self-appointed critic of Professor Pearson, lay in Pearson's choice to mourn not having been born into a more promising world versus Roosevelt's decision to live in the very best of times. Every time and every place—every possible circumstance—offer ample sources of interest, excitement, and enjoyment, of opportunity and of profit, provided that you are prepared to explore and exploit those sources. Begin by deciding that *your* time and *your* place offer more possibility than you could ever begin to exhaust. Simply choose to live in the best of times.

■

## Lesson 70
## Refuse Red Tape

"Don't bother me with a letter. I haven't time to read it."
~ Assistant Secretary of the Navy Roosevelt to a ship dealer
on the eve of the Spanish-American War

As the United States prepared to go to war with Spain over the issue of Cuban independence, Theodore Roosevelt, in his capacity as assistant secretary of the navy, was given the task of buying up available merchant vessels for quick conversion to armed U.S. Navy cruisers. Charles R. Flint, a dealer in such merchant craft, called on Roosevelt and offered him the Brazilian merchantman *Nictheroy*. Before Flint could begin his pitch, Roosevelt cut him off, explaining that he had already thoroughly researched the ship and knew all about it. His only question to Flint was "What is the price?" The dealer replied that it was half a million dollars, to which Roosevelt responded, "I will take her." That is when Flint offered to write him a letter with the particulars of the sale. All Roosevelt wanted, however, was the ship.

Only after the deal was made did Roosevelt draft a letter of agreement, which Flint marveled at as "one of the most concise and at the same time one of the cleverest contracts" he had ever seen. Roosevelt specified that the vessel be "delivered under her own steam at a specific point and within a specific period." That was it. Flint observed: "In one sentence he thus covered all that might have been set forth in pages and pages of specifications. For the vessel *had* to be in first-class condition to make the time scheduled in the contract!"

Roosevelt did not merely cut through red tape, he refused to deal with it altogether. This he accomplished by simply and directly taking action. Just as he compressed the purchasing process into a single act, so he provided all of the protection a contract offered by concentrating the required guarantees into deeds instead of words. Rather than creating a complex set of written promises and conditions, he instead specified a delivery schedule intended to prove the condition of the merchandise. He had need of performance, not promises.

**The American historian and diplomat** Henry Adams called Theodore Roosevelt "pure act." It was as apt a description of the man as has ever been offered. At his characteristic best, TR totally removed the customary gap between word and deed. He devised remarkable ways to transform thought directly into action with virtually no steps or empty space in between. As an administrator, he represents a model of efficiency that continues to reward study today.

■

*Lesson 71*
## Failure Is an Option

> "It is hard to fail; but it is worse never to have tried to succeed."
> ~Speech, Chicago, April 10, 1899

Throughout his life and throughout his presidency, Theodore Roosevelt established clear goals and then strove mightily to achieve them, but he always attached greater importance to the striving rather than the goal. Having reached the goal was an achievement, over and done with once attained, but striving was a way of life, never finished, and therefore infinitely more valuable.

**Some people need goals,** while others are daunted by them. To some, a goal promises success. To others, it warns of the possibility of failure and therefore reinforces the inertia that retards individual and collective action alike. Of course it is important to plan. Goals and the objectives necessary to reach those goals should be painted as bright red lines: perfectly clear. Just make sure you also give the members of your organization the option to fail and the space to recover from their failures. Never let the setting of goals eclipse the crucial importance of trying. Make this mistake and you will hobble, not enable, your enterprise.

■

*Lesson 72*
## Value Character "Far Above"

> "Bodily vigor is good, and vigor of intellect is even better, but far above both is character."
>
> ~ "Character and Success," in *The Outlook*, March 31, 1900

What "counts"—what finally determines worth—is not money, not "bodily vigor," and not even "vigor of intellect," Theodore Roosevelt explained to an audience at Galena, Illinois, on April 27, 1900. "It is character," he declared, "that counts in a nation as in a man."

Just a month earlier he had published a popular article on character in *The Outlook*, and it was a word he used over and over again throughout his life and career. Yet, like so many concepts that form a core belief, *character* eludes precise definition. TR nevertheless took a stab at it, loosely associating *character* with a combination of intelligence, unselfishness, courage, and decency—and with a persistent unwillingness to "let well enough alone."

"In the great battle of life," he wrote in *The Outlook*, "no brilliancy of intellect, no perfection of bodily development, will count when weighed in the balance against that assemblage of virtues, active and passive, of moral qualities, which we group together under the name of character."

*Character.* For Roosevelt, the word was a magnet, irresistibly attracting to itself a host of other words: "the watchwords of honesty, decency, fair-dealing, and common sense"—words he used in a speech at the New York State Fair on September 7, 1903. Back in August of 1890, in the *North American Review*, he had included "not only such qualities as honesty and truthfulness, but courage, perseverance and self-reliance."

Year after year, he worked at his definition. For, as Roosevelt saw it, *character* was one of those all-important ideals that cried out to be made real. "If a man does not have an ideal and try to live up to it," he wrote to his son Kermit (in a 1915 letter quoted by Joseph Bucklin Bishop in his *Theodore Roosevelt and His Time*), "then he becomes a mean, base, and sordid creature, no matter how successful."

Whatever words *character* summoned up, it could not be simply and definitively pinned down and quantified. It was, as he explained in an article published in the *Ladies' Home Journal* in January 1917, the quality that enabled you to master your soul, and "Unless a man is master of his soul, all other kinds of mastery amount to little."

**It is often said** that if you want to succeed in business of any kind, you must speak the universal language of business, which is money. The implication of this assertion is that no other language finally counts. TR taught that, on the contrary, the only language that finally "counts" is not just non-monetary, but fundamentally non-quantifiable. It is *character* and all the non-material qualities and values the word and concept summon up.

Whatever else *character* is—and it seems to be many things—it is the essence of humanity at its best, and while the surface of business is undeniably a complex flow of goods, services, and funds, the force that drives this circulation is both first and last human. No business does business with a business. All business is conducted, finally, from one person to another. At the core of every transaction, therefore, is character: its presence, its absence, its abundance, its scarcity.

■

## Lesson 73
## Get Action

"Get action; do things; be sane."

~Remark to a former Rough Rider, 1902,
quoted in Edmund Morris, *Theodore Rex*, 2001

Frustrated by the inactivity of the Fifty-seventh Congress, which dragged its feet when it came to casting the presidential agenda in the form of new laws, Roosevelt exploded at one of his former troops who had come to visit. "Get action; do things; be sane," he exhorted him, then went on to advise, "Don't fritter away your time. . . . Be somebody; get action."

We don't know what the full context of this exchange was, and it is impossible to tell whether Roosevelt's advice was useful to the veteran or not. What we do know was that everything Roosevelt said or did was always aimed at eliciting action. Communication that failed in this was just so much frittering away of time that proved you were nobody.

> **Every word you utter** or effort you make in business should be directed toward producing a tangible result. Setting out with the intention of getting action and doing things is the only sane course for a leader to take.

■

*Lesson 74*
## Draw a Starting Line

> "The first requisite of a good citizen in this Republic of ours is that he shall be able and willing to pull his weight."
>
> ~Speech, New York City, November 11, 1902

In his inaugural address, President John F. Kennedy made stirringly clear precisely what he expected of every American citizen. "Ask not," he exhorted, "what your country can do for you; ask what you can do for your country." The phrase was lofty and ringing, but it was also daunting in that it seemed to ask an awful lot of ordinary people. Some fifty-nine years earlier, Theodore Roosevelt had put a similar expectation in homelier and therefore less overwhelming terms, asking no more but no less than that each citizen "be able and willing to pull his weight."

> **Many executives and managers** fret over "inspiring" the members of their organization. Motivation, persuasion, and inspiration are, without doubt, important leadership tasks, but as with anything else you build, building inspired performance should start at the level of foundation, not in the middle and certainly not at the top. Before you utter high-flying words

proposing impossible levels of achievement, draw a baseline
that all will invariably understand and accept: the willingness
and the ability to contribute to the advancement of the
organization rather than to its collective dead weight. Every
race requires a starting line. Draw one.

*Lesson 75*
## Let the Situation Command

"In my judgment the situation imperatively requires that you meet
upon the common plane of the necessities of the public."
~ To principals in the coal strike conference he convened at the
White House, October 3, 1902

As the great anthracite coal strike of 1902 threatened to create a
winter coal famine, leaving millions of families without winter
heating fuel, Theodore Roosevelt took the unprecedented step of
offering the federal government as a neutral arbitrator in a labor
dispute (see Lesson 123, "Protect *Your* Flock"). Wary about
appearing to side with either the miners (and their union) or the
mine owners, the president deftly removed himself from the position
of having to compel *either* side to submit themselves to the
arbitration. Instead, he put "the situation" in command.

"We are," he explained to both sides and to the nation, "upon
the threshold of winter, with an already existing coal famine, the
future terrors of which we can hardly yet appreciate. The evil
possibilities are so far-reaching, so appalling, that it seems to me that
you are not only justified in sinking, but required to sink, for the
time being any tenacity as to your respective claims in the matter at
issue between you." Notice the passive sentence structure—"you are
required," not "I require you"—by which President Roosevelt

removed himself from command, compulsion, or threat. When he returned to using the active voice, it was not he who made any demand, but "the situation." "In my judgment," Roosevelt declared, "the situation imperatively requires that you meet upon the common plane of the necessities of the public."

*Address issues, not egos* is a valuable principle of leadership. Your objective should always be to fix problems rather than to try to fix people. Things—issues, opportunities, difficulties— have no egos to promote or to protect. They have no private motives or hidden agendas. They have nothing to gain and nothing to lose. It stands to reason, therefore, that things can be fixed far more readily than people. Whenever possible, therefore, use problems, issues, opportunities, difficulties—in short, use the situation, to prompt, require, or command the action you desire. Take yourself and your ego out of the equation. Define the *situation*, and make *it*, not *you*, the driver of purest, most neutral, yet most imperative necessity.

■

## Lesson 76
## Serve No Dead Words

> "The Constitution was made for the people and not the people for
> the Constitution."
> ~ To Congressman James E. Watson, during the coal strike of 1902

Raised, like so many other Americans of his era, on the Bible, Theodore Roosevelt well knew Saint Paul's counsel to the Corinthians about the error of preaching the letter rather than the spirit of faith. The "letter killeth," Paul wrote, "but the spirit giveth life." In a similar vein, the president replied to Congressman James E. Watson, who protested his preparations to call in the

U.S. Army to take over the Pennsylvania coalfields if the strike could not be ended in time to avert a critical shortage of coal to warm American homes in the approaching winter. "I bid you pay no heed to any other authority, no heed to a writ from a judge, or anything excepting my commands," Roosevelt had ordered General John M. Schofield.

Aghast at this order, Watson pressed the president: "What about the Constitution of the United States?"

Roosevelt laid firm hands on his fellow Republican's shoulders. He spoke to him softly but firmly: "The Constitution was made for the people and not the people for the Constitution."

**No successful company** thrives in the service of "company policy." When policy fails to serve the company, policy must yield to people. You are the one who must make it yield.

■

*Lesson 77*
## Apply Rules Equally, Consistently, and Absolutely

"No man is above the law and no man is below it; nor do we ask any man's permission when we require him to obey it."

~Annual message to Congress, December 7, 1903

It is always dangerous to become a slave to "company policy" by allowing it to stand in for creative judgment when the situation offers new challenges, threats, or opportunities. Roosevelt believed that "order without liberty" was destructive. Yet, as he wrote in *The Great Adventure* (1918), "Order without liberty and liberty without order are equally destructive."

Leadership cannot be exclusively a matter of improvisation. Rules—including "company policy"—must be applied unless there is an overwhelming reason to suspend or alter their application. In no case, however, are they to be applied unequally, inconsistently, or randomly. Apply the rules of your enterprise equally to all, including yourself. Never ask that they be followed. Require it, and require it without apology.

■

*Lesson 78*
## Real Power Is Power You Really Use

"I had much rather be a real President for three years and a half than a figurehead for seven years and a half."
~ To his friend, British historian and statesman
Sir George Otto Trevelyan, May 1904

In 1902, Venezuelan president Cipriano Castro refused demands from Great Britain and Germany to pay commercial debts owed to these nations as well as damages suffered by Britons, Germans, and other European citizens during the recent Venezuelan civil war. In response to the refusal, on December 7, 1902, Britain and Germany united in issuing ultimatums threatening a naval blockade, which was in fact imposed two days later. Although the blockade loomed as a prelude to invasion, Cipriano Castro continued to rebuff British and German demands, confident that President Roosevelt would stand by the Monroe Doctrine, which, since President James Monroe had promulgated it in 1823, had pledged the United States to defend the Americas against all foreign incursions and attempts at colonization. President Roosevelt, however, believed that Venezuela had a responsibility to honor its debts, and he accepted British and German assurances that the blockade was an attempt to enforce international law and not a prelude to the seizure of territory. He therefore allowed the blockade to proceed without U.S. interference—until, that is, blockading vessels sank two Venezuelan ships and bombarded the coast, even after Cipriano Castro had finally agreed to international arbitration. At this, Roosevelt ordered the U.S. fleet to assemble near the blockading force, whereupon the European creditors and Venezuela signed an agreement on February 13, 1903, committing nearly a third of Venezuela's customs duties to settling claims in return for the removal of the blockade.

Thus, in large part thanks to a quiet but firm demonstration of U.S. force—"big stick diplomacy"—the Venezuelan Crisis was resolved. It gave rise, a year later, to the so-called Roosevelt Corollary of the Monroe Doctrine, announced in the president's annual message to Congress for 1904:

All that this country desires is to see the neighboring countries stable, orderly, and prosperous. Any country whose people conduct themselves well can count upon our hearty friendship. If a nation shows that it knows how to act with reasonable efficiency and decency in social and political matters, if it keeps order and pays its obligations, it need fear no interference from the United States. Chronic wrongdoing, or an impotence which results in a general loosening of the ties of civilized society, may in America, as elsewhere, ultimately require intervention by some civilized nation, and in the Western Hemisphere the adherence of the United States to the Monroe Doctrine may force the United States, however reluctantly, in flagrant cases of such wrongdoing or impotence, to the exercise of an international police power.

Some welcomed the president's assertion of the nation's right to intervene to "stabilize" the economic policies of states in the Caribbean and Central America if they claimed inability to pay their international debts, praising it as a noble means of upholding the Monroe Doctrine and preventing European interference in the Western hemisphere. Others, however, condemned it as a transparent excuse for blatant hemispherical imperialism. Many of those who saw the direction of TR's policy before he announced it in December 1904 warned the president that it might cost him the election. Roosevelt responded to them as he did to Trevelyan, explaining that he would "much rather be a real President for three years and a half than a figurehead for seven years and a half."

**Power is theoretical until** it is exercised. Power becomes real only when it is used. Reality always carries more risk than theory, but theory remedies no wrong and exploits no opportunity. To actually lead is to actually exercise power.

■

*Lesson 79*
## Fix Things, Not People

"War with the evil; but show no spirit of malignity toward the man who may be responsible for the evil. Put it out of his power to do wrong."

~Speech, Oyster Bay, New York, July 4, 1906

Theodore Roosevelt was a law-and-order man. Not only did he make an early name for himself as an effective public servant with his dynamic stint as president of the New York City Police Board, but, as a Progressive president, he relied on the law to rein in what he saw as the predatory excesses of big business. His strong belief in self-reliance ended where individualism threatened to become predatory lawlessness and anarchy. More than any preceding occupant of the White House, he advocated an extensive and vigorous federal role in the national life.

There is no question that TR saw himself at "war with . . . evil." His strategy in this war, however, had far less to do with crime and punishment—with punishing the wrongdoer—than it had with creating a system of government and law, infused with a collective spirit of the public good, that put wrongdoing "out of [the] power" of those who would do wrong. His objective was to prevent or, even better, to preclude wrong before the fact rather than punish it afterward. To achieve this, Roosevelt combined federal oversight and regulation (often enacted through direct executive order when Congress proved unwilling to pass the laws he wanted) with the moral authority of the bully pulpit of the presidency to prevent monopolistic and predatory business practices and to promote conservation rather than seek to punish the predators and the exploiters after they had committed their destructive acts.

**Problems are part of** any endeavor. The leader of an organization has a choice of attempting to resolve problems either by addressing those who cause them or by addressing the problems themselves. As President Roosevelt understood, it is nearly impossible to fix people, but it is very feasible and highly effective to fix problems. Tell people what you want of them. Discover ways to motivate and guide them. But understand, as TR did, that the most efficient way of warring with evil is to design systems that put bad things beyond the power of those who would do bad things. Address issues rather than personalities. Fix things, not people.

*Lesson 80*
## How Not to Sweat the Small Stuff

> "It would be nonsense to refuse to allow a person to use the term
> 'Castile' unless the soap was made in Spain."
>
> ~Letter to Secretary of Agriculture James Wilson,
> September 12, 1906

President Roosevelt is justly famous for having championed passage of the Pure Food and Drug Act along with a host of other legislation promoting food and drug safety and protecting consumers with truth-in-labeling regulations. He insisted that the laws be rigorously enforced, but, as with everything he did, TR drew the line at upholding the letter of the law to the point that the letter killed the very spirit of the legislation. For him, the divide between productive enforcement and destructive enforcement was bright and clear. Zeal must end where nonsense begins.

When Thomas E. Wilson, who founded and ran the giant Chicago meatpacker Wilson and Company, complained about a Department of Agriculture order that his company remove the word *Bologna* from its sausages, President Roosevelt intervened. "Mr. Wilson's . . . complaint is that of being required to leave off the word 'Bologna' from sausages, on the ground that it is not made in Bologna," Roosevelt wrote to his secretary of agriculture. "I think on this he is right." The president went on to justify his opinion:

> Bologna sausages are not commonly understood to be made
> in Bologna any more than Castile soap is understood to be
> made in Spain. It would be nonsense to refuse to allow a
> person to use the term "Castile" unless the soap was made in
> Spain. So it would seem to me to be nonsense to refuse to
> allow people to use the word "Bologna" before "sausage" if, as
> a matter of fact, it is the same sausage as people call Bologna
> sausage. Not one in a thousand persons knows where
> Bologna is—and I am not personally that one.

Common usage, common sense, and universal analogy directed the president's thinking. There was no productive benefit to be created by interfering with commerce over a nonsensical technicality. And so meatpacker Wilson was set free to sell his bologna as bologna.

> **Write and enforce rules** to create a benefit for the enterprise. When compliance ceases to produce such a benefit, alter the rules or reinterpret them. Regulation and the enforcement of regulation for the mere sake of regulation is at best non-productive and at worst, frankly destructive. Investing time, energy, and cash in non-productivity is nonsense, whereas the decision to avoid committing to nonsense is self-evident. You know what decision to make.

■

*Lesson 81*
## Create Excellence

> "Success—the real success—does not depend upon the position
> you hold, but upon how you carry yourself in that position."
> ~Address, University of Cambridge, United Kingdom, May 26, 1910

TR rose from state assemblyman to New York's top cop, New York's governor, assistant secretary of the navy, vice president, and president of the United States. It must have been difficult for him to resist measuring his success in life by the upward magnificence of the arc of his career. Yet, although Roosevelt was undeniably competitive, he was no mere scorekeeper. His objective in life was less to rise from position to position than it was to achieve excellence within whatever position he occupied. Quality rather than quantity of achievement was the standard by which he measured his professional life as well as the careers of others.

**Your rise from position** to position is a measure of your personal progress. It is gratifying, to be sure, but, in the end, it is steps up a ladder, an achievement of value chiefly limited to yourself. In contrast, your performance at each level, in each position you hold, extends your achievement out from your ego and into the world. The service you perform is the benefit you build for your enterprise. You can create this level of excellence in whatever position at whatever level you hold at a particular time and place. Bear this in mind: *Theodore Roosevelt performed as assemblyman and police commissioner with the same intensity he exercised in discharging the very highest office in the land.*

## Lesson 82
## Give Everyone a Square Deal

"When I say I am for the square deal, I mean not merely that I stand for fair play under the present rules of the game, but that I stand for having those rules changed so as to work for a more substantial equality of opportunity and of reward for equally good service."

~Speech, Osawatomie, Kansas, August 31, 1910

TR launched his third-party bid for the White House on a campaign for what he called the "Square Deal," which he defined succinctly in a number of speeches, including one he delivered at Osawatomie, Kansas, in 1910.

At its most basic, his concept of the Square Deal was built on the most self-evident and appealing of commonsense notions. Americans had the right to enjoy equality of compensation and equality of opportunity (equal pay for equal work). The problem,

TR saw, was that the "rules of the game" as currently set down–the law as it existed–did not promote this straightforward, even self-evident concept. Because existing law was out of step with common sense–the Square Deal expressed a virtually universal notion of justice–Roosevelt reasoned that the law had to be changed. Since neither major political party, Democratic or Republican, seemed willing to change it, he resolved to offer voters a third party alternative. Theodore Roosevelt's objective in this was simple: to do the right thing by introducing (as he wrote years later, in 1917) a "square deal for every man! That is the only safe motto for the United States."

> **When it comes to** issues of fairness, especially where opportunity and reward are concerned, complex philosophies and formulas are rarely more valid than the most basic common sense. Endeavor to give everyone a square deal: "equality of opportunity and of reward for equally good service."

■

*Lesson 83*
## Practice the Art of the Fait Accompli

> "I took the [Panama Canal Zone], started the canal, and then left Congress–not to debate the canal, but to debate me. But while the debate goes on the canal does too."
> ~Speech at Berkeley, California, March 23, 1911

In his 1913 *An Autobiography*, Theodore Roosevelt explained the decision he made to "take" the Panama Canal Zone as a way to convert what he described as "nearly four hundred years" of talk about building an "Isthmus canal" (a conversation that had been under way since the days of Balboa) into action. In 1901, he saw an opportunity to act by approving the Hay-Paunceforte Treaty with

Great Britain, which, along with negotiations with the French Panama Company, gave the United States possession of an as-yet vaguely defined permanently neutral "canal zone" through which it had the right to carve a canal. When surveys determined that the best place for the canal zone was specifically across the Isthmus of Panama, President Roosevelt immediately ordered Secretary of State John Hay to conclude in 1903 the Hay-Herrán Treaty with the government of Colombia, which at the time possessed Panama. When, roiled with rebellion, the Colombian Senate rejected the Hay-Herrán Treaty in 1903, Roosevelt employed Philippe Bunau-Varilla, a French engineer who had worked for the French Panama Canal Company (which had tried and failed to build a canal in the 1880s), to take Panama independent through a bloodless coup. The provisional government of the new Panamanian state commissioned Bunau-Varilla minister plenipotentiary, with the power to conclude the Hay–Bunau-Varilla Treaty, giving the United States the right to build a canal through a U.S.-controlled canal zone.

"The time for hesitation on our part had passed," Roosevelt observed in his 1913 *An Autobiography*. The need for the canal–for "easy and speedy communication by sea between the Atlantic and the Pacific"–was, he believed, "immediate." Had he "acted otherwise than [he] did," he wrote, he would have been guilty of "betrayal of the interests of the United States, indifference to the interests of Panama, and recreancy to the interests of the world at large."

At the time, Congress was not so sure. Even after the Senate approved the Hay–Bunau-Varilla Treaty, debate ebbed and flowed over both the wisdom and the justice–not to mention, the legality under international law–of what the president proposed. Roosevelt chose not to interfere with the debate. Instead, with the treaty in hand, he personally pushed the Panama Canal forward, and soon it had acquired the irresistible momentum of an accomplished fact or, more precisely, a fact progressing toward accomplishment.

> **Words can be powerful,** but the most powerful word is weak
> alongside a fact in motion or a fact accomplished.

■

*Lesson 84*
## What to Do with Power

"The presidency should be a powerful office, and the President a
powerful man, who will take every advantage of it . . ."
~Letter to his sister Corinne, June 26, 1908

"I enjoy being President," Theodore Roosevelt wrote to his son
Kermit on October 2, 1903. Not everyone who had preceded him in
the office felt the same way, and, except for Abraham Lincoln, no
president before him used the power of the presidency so fully. As
some said of Lincoln, so some said—and still say—of TR: *He did not
scruple to cross the line from chief executive to dictator.*

We will not debate this opinion here, not in the case of Lincoln
and not in the instance of Roosevelt. Instead, consider a fact that is
beyond debate: Theodore Roosevelt elevated the executive order,
hitherto used chiefly for occasional narrow and usually more or less
ceremonial purposes, into a means of governing that was a bold
alternative to legislation passed by the houses of Congress. He
issued a total of 1,091 executive orders during his seven-and-a-half
years in office. Although Woodrow Wilson would issued 1,791
(many of them relating to complex and urgent matters in the
prosecution of World War I) and his fifth cousin Franklin Delano
Roosevelt would hand down a staggering 3,723 (in the course of
nearly twelve years as president, during the Depression and World
War II), TR's volume nearly eclipsed the *combined* total, 1,259, of the
twenty-five presidents who preceded him.

> **What to do with power?** Theodore Roosevelt would not have hesitated to answer. *Use it. Use it. And use it some more.*

■

*Lesson 85*
## Fight Majority Misrule

"Whenever there is tyranny by the majority I shall certainly fight it."

~ Speech, St. Louis, March 28, 1912

As President Roosevelt was well aware, the United States is not a democracy, but a democratic republic, in which the people elect officials less to represent them than to intelligently interpret and implement their best interests. As Roosevelt saw it, republicanism often entailed protecting the nation against the transitory will of the majority when he judged that will to be ill advised or just plain wrong.

Ultimately, TR found himself having to fight what he judged to be the misguided will of the majority of his own Republican Party, which had become, in his view, hyper-conservative in the domestic as well as the international arenas. He therefore chose to run in 1912 as the presidential candidate of the Progressive (some called it Bull Moose) Party, and many of his campaign speeches, such the one he gave in St. Louis on March 28, 1912, focused on fighting "tyranny by the majority."

> **One of the most** difficult judgments any leader must make is where to separate the leadership function from the "followership" function. Some leaders are simply autocratic and take little or no interest in the opinions, let alone the will, of

the majority or, for that matter, the minority. Others see themselves as facilitators, whose function is to solicit, comprehend, and implement the input of the members of the organization. Just where you define yourself along this spectrum depends variously and in part on the nature of your organization, the nature of your business, and the nature of your own nature. These variables aside, however, your best option is to define your role by emulating Roosevelt. Decide that, as a leader, you must be a representative. But just as TR understood that his constituency was neither the majority nor the minority, but the nation, so you, as leader of the enterprise, must represent the enterprise and make decisions aimed at creating the greatest benefit for it. Build your leadership on this foundation and, in the long run, you will create the greatest benefit for all stakeholders in the organization.

■

*Lesson 86*
## How to Lead a Self-Governing Enterprise

"All of us, you and I, all of us together, want to rule ourselves, and we don't wish to have any body of outsiders rule us. That is what free government means."

~Speech, St. Louis, March 28, 1912

Theodore Roosevelt was a strong believer in government, the object of which, he explained in *The New Nationalism* (1910), was "the welfare of the people." The government he wanted, however, was self-government. As he told an audience at Jamestown, Virginia, on April 26, 1907, "Men can never escape being governed. Either they must govern themselves or they must submit to being governed by others."

Clearly, the better choice was self-government. For a government to work without force and compulsion, authority had to come from within. We "want to rule ourselves, and we don't wish to have any body of outsiders rule us." Yet self-government was certainly not without stumbling blocks, all of which, Roosevelt believed, came from a misunderstanding of precisely what *self-government* meant.

Many people misunderstood *self* as a synonym for *individual* or, more to the point, for *me*. Roosevelt, however, defined *self* as "All of us, you and I, all of us together." Thus *self*-government was really *collective* government, a government in which all action must be for the common good, the collective self, not for the particular benefit of this or that individual. It is the leader's job to direct, guide, and moderate self-government to ensure that the collective self is being well served. The art of leading a self-governing organization is in never allowing the people to feel that authority—government—is being forced on them from outside. "We, the people, rule ourselves," Roosevelt continued his St. Louis speech, "and what we really want from our representatives is that they shall manage the government for us along the lines we lay down, and shall do this with efficiency and in good faith."

**In any organization,** self-government is more difficult to execute and manage than authoritarian government. Why, then, bother with self-government? Because it offers very significant advantages. It leverages human resources by creating a collaborative environment that gives everyone a voice in the conduct of the organization and a stake in the outcome of everything the organization does. In the self-governing organization, creative and executive powers are multiplied by the number of members involved, and the burden on any one member is proportionately reduced. In the self-governing organization, motivation and commitment tend to be increased, while self-serving agendas are reduced. The price you pay as a leader is the effort required to reconfigure your role from absolute commander to authoritative facilitator, and from autocratic director to sure-footed manager.

■

## *Lesson 87*
## Think Big Picture, Then Think Even Bigger

"I see no reason for believing that Russia is more advanced than Germany as regards international ethics, and Japan, with all her politeness and her veneer of western civilization, is at heart delighted to attack any and every western nation whenever the chances come and there is an opportunity for Japan to gain what she desires with reasonable safety. If Germany is smashed, it is perfectly possible that later she will have to be supported as a bulwark against [Russia] by the nations of Western Europe."

~ *The Outlook*, September 23, 1914

The Great War, as World War I was known in the days before World War II, was only into its second month of full-scale combat when former president Roosevelt wrote these words. At the time, the vast majority of Americans counted themselves lucky to be taking no part in what many of them called the "European War," and American sentiment concerning the belligerents varied from support for Germany and its allies (this came chiefly from anti-English Irish immigrants and from German immigrants), to support for Britain, France, and its ally Russia, to general condemnation of everyone involved, to total blissful indifference. If any one of these public and political sentiments dominated the United States in the autumn of 1914, however, it was the sense that Germany had united with Austria-Hungary in aggression impossible to rationalize and that "the Allies"—France, Britain, and Russia—were making a justifiable response. As for Japan, it had joined the Allies against Germany and played what is today a little-remembered but nevertheless significant role in denying to German transports and warships the sea lanes of the South Pacific and Indian Oceans.

Theodore Roosevelt understood all this. Unlike many of his fellow Americans, top political leaders included, he followed the developing war with great intensity and interest. He understood the prevailing American sentiments, and he disagreed with them. For what the former president understood most of all was, whatever horrors the Great War was visiting upon the world today, it was also creating the geopolitical world of tomorrow. He looked beyond the conventional "wisdom," which was deeply colored by cultural biases and assumptions and, most of all, by immediate political and military interests. What he saw, with remarkable clarity, were the conditions that would create a *second* world war and, beyond this, even those circumstances that would give rise to the Cold War afterward.

Some of Roosevelt's more superficial commentators have criticized him as a jingoist, who focused narrowly on the aggrandizement of the United States. This is both unfair and inaccurate; for he was, in fact, an internationalist who saw far and wide, not only geographically, but geopolitically—in the dimension of historical time as well as that of geographical space. Looking beyond current diplomatic and political expedience and beyond cultural clichés, TR penetrated to the level of motive and national self-interest, concluding that it was a mistake to assume that the behavior of a nation in 1914 was an accurate indication, let alone a guarantee, of its behavior in the years and decades to come. He not only possessed the informed imagination to see the big picture over time, but the courage and integrity to express what he imagined, even when it might be intensely unpopular to do so.

**You must act in the present,** of course, but never assume that present circumstances will hold for eternity. Even as you tend to your business day to day, exercise your big-picture imagination. Endeavor to see beneath the surface, not on the cynical assumption that people and organizations are invariably deceptive, but in the knowledge that the motives driving individuals and enterprises in any environment or marketplace are inevitably dynamic and subject to the most radical realignment through time. Successful leadership is based on formulating winning tactics for the present based on a strategy designed both to anticipate and to meet an ever-evolving big picture. Unquestioned assumptions and the reliance on received wisdom and clichés stand between short-term tactics and long-term strategy.

■

*Lesson 88*
## Speak the Language of Business

"No wise or generous soul will be content with a success which can be expressed only in dollars, but the soul which spurns all consideration of dollars usually drags down both itself and other souls into the gulf of pitiful failure."

~ *Ladies' Home Journal,* October 1916

Money did not top Theodore Roosevelt's hierarchy of values, but it nevertheless figured—and figured prominently—in that list. He believed, as he told an audience in Berkeley, California, in 1911, that it was "a false statement, and therefore . . . a disservice to the cause of morality, to say that money does not count." For proof, he cited reality: "If [a man] has not got it he will find that it does count tremendously."

Ideals, integrity, courage, nobility of aspiration—all essential qualities to greatness as a leader—will not fill the belly, pay the rent, or prosper a business. Money is the universal language of business. Whatever other languages you speak in leading your enterprise—those of ideals, integrity, courage, and nobility of aspiration among them—you must speak first and last the language of business. No one knew this better than Theodore Roosevelt.

■

*Lesson 89*
## Don't Be Too Smart

"I have only a second rate brain, but I think I have a capacity for action."

~ Quoted in Owen Wister, *Roosevelt: The Story of a Friendship*, 1930

A true friend is one to whom you can reveal your most brutal and unsparing of self-assessments. It is doubtful, however, that Owen Wister or anyone else who knew TR would agree with rating his intelligence as anything less than first rate. Nevertheless, Roosevelt made his point. An effective leader had less need for a massive mind than for a massive "capacity for action."

The phrase is significant. It was not *energy*, or *willingness*, or *eagerness*, or *ability*, but "capacity." The word encompassed absolutely everything required to take, lead, order, or direct *action*. As Roosevelt saw it, this capacity was the key faculty required to lead, and while many other minds might be finer than his, few people possessed an ampler capacity for action.

Leadership is not a contemplative art. It is above all things an *executive* function. This implies that the business of leadership is primarily *execution*—a matter of action more than of contemplation. Whatever a leader examines, studies, reviews, reads, thinks, or discusses, he or she must bear uppermost in mind the clear object of taking action, of converting input in a timely and efficient manner into productive output. The process, mostly a matter of thought, is essential, of course, provided it is not allowed to compromise the capacity for action.

■

*Lesson 90*
## Don't Just Lead, Manage

"The bulk of government is not legislation but administration."
~Quoted by John Morton Blum,
*The Republican Roosevelt,* 1954

History remembers—and celebrates—many leaders and very few managers, but Theodore Roosevelt, although always mindful of his legacy and place in history, understood that the work of governing was less legislative leadership than it was administrative management. Acute consciousness of this fact was a principal driver of one of his most ambitious legislative initiatives: civil service reform. As a leader, Roosevelt wanted to purge corruption from government, especially corruption in the form of to-the-winner-belong-the-spoils political patronage. As a manager, he wanted to create an administrative apparatus staffed not by political hacks but by competent professionals who had been hired on their merits rather than on the basis of some favor owed by an elected official.

> **Whether you call** yourself (or aspire to call yourself) CEO, president, or vice president, your leadership enables, even as it is enabled by, competent, efficient, responsive, proactive administrative management. The most visionary business leader climbs the mountain on a path maintained by sound management.

■

*Lesson 91*
## Be Utterly and Completely Present

"The world seemed blotted out. . . . I felt that, for the time being, I was the sole object of his interest and concern."
~ Amy Belle (Cheney) Clinton, to Roosevelt biographer
Hermann Hagedorn, January 17, 1949

When she visited the White House and met President Roosevelt, Amy Belle Cheney was a debutante–she would marry in 1908–but she carried the memory of the meeting lifelong, describing its effect to Roosevelt biographer Hermann Hagedorn some four decades later.

Roosevelt's most important biographer, Edmund Morris, points out that the president's ability to focus on the likes of Amy Belle Cheney was not romantic or sexual. It was, rather, a matter of compelling personal style. He made virtually everyone he spoke with feel this way. Amy Belle seems to have understood this, too. Although she told Hagedorn that Roosevelt made her feel like "the sole object of his interest and concern," she modified that observation with the phrase "for the time being." This is key. Roosevelt was not merely warm and charming–though he was these things–he also possessed the valuable capacity for being utterly and completely present in the moment, offering himself

[ 153 ]

wholly (for that moment) to the person he was with. This made him an incredibly powerful, persuasive, and memorable presence.

**It was no mean** feat for the president of the United States, pressed for attention on all sides and at all times, to focus wholly and sincerely on a single person and a single conversation at a particular time. You may not be chief executive of the nation, but it's hardly easy for you, goaded by a vibrating smartphone, inundated by emails, and assaulted by text messages, to keep yourself in the moment. Not easy. But absolutely critical. Face to face or on the phone, stop multitasking and, "for the time being," ensure that the other person feels he or she is the sole object of your interest.

■

# Lead the Political Life

*Lesson 92*
## Take the Through Route to Understanding

> "The reason that he knew so much about everything . . . was that wherever he went he got right in with the people."
> ~ William Wingate Sewall, *Bill Sewall's Story of TR*, 1919

Roosevelt met Bill Sewall early in 1878. A Maine lumberman, Sewall hosted Roosevelt during the young man's vacation in the woods of Aroostook County. Sewall expected to be dealing with a rich New York "swell." Instead, he was amazed at how TR succeeded in charming the backwoodsmen. "Theodore enjoyed them immensely," Sewall wrote. "He told me after he left the camp how glad he was that he had met them. He said that he could read about such things, but here he had got first-hand accounts of backwoods life from the men who had lived it and knew what they were talking about."

Bill Sewall immediately understood two things about Theodore Roosevelt.

First, TR made a natural connection with people, regardless of how apparently different they were from him. He was empathetic. Deeply interested in the lives and concerns of others, he watched and he listened and he appreciated. He looked down on no one. He found something to admire in just about everyone.

Second, Roosevelt loved to read, but he craved even more the totally unfiltered, unmediated contact with reality—"first-hand."

**Look away from the computer.** Get up from behind your desk. Walk out of your office. Watch, listen to, and appreciate the members of your organization. Talk to them about their work.

More importantly, listen to what they tell you about their work. What do they need? What are their objectives? What problems do they face? What opportunities do they perceive? Enjoy conversing with them. Resolve to find something to admire in each of them. Do all this, and you will know everything knowable about the enterprise you lead.

■

### Lesson 93
## Be Afraid, but Act with Courage

"There were all kinds of things of which I was afraid at first, ranging from grizzly bears to 'mean' horses and gun-fighters; but by acting as if I was not afraid I gradually ceased to be afraid."

~ *An Autobiography*, 1913

It is not surprising that a number of actors become politicians and very successful politicians at that, Ronald Reagan and Arnold Schwarzenegger among them. More surprising, perhaps, is that politicians rarely become professional actors. Maybe that's because it is difficult to come down from a stage bounded by nothing but a few state or national borders to one enclosed by wings and footlights.

Never a professional actor, Theodore Roosevelt was an earnest public leader who nevertheless knew how to put on a very persuasive show. He was an actor in all but name, and what he learned early on when he (New York "dude" that he was) ventured out West to run a Badlands ranch, was that if he played a part convincingly enough, he could even convince himself.

**Authenticity is a vastly overrated** quality in leaders. Fears, self-doubt, worry—these may be uppermost in your mind at any one time, but needed action cannot wait for you to overcome your fears or to feel better. Borrow the lesson Roosevelt learned. Go ahead and be afraid. Just act as if you are courageous. In the short run, this charade will help you get things done. In the long run, it may actually change your feelings.

■

*Lesson 94*
## Seek Support

> "I am a Republican, pure and simple, . . . and certainly no man,
> nor yet any ring or clique, can do my thinking for me."
> ~ Campaign letter for New York State Assembly speaker, 1883

After winning reelection to the New York State Assembly in 1883, Roosevelt mounted a campaign for selection as assembly speaker. He began by sending each of the Republican assemblymen-elect a letter introducing himself. To those who asked for more information, he gave the varied and dazzling particulars of his background— Harvard educated, already a dynamic veteran of the assembly, and the owner of a ranch in the Dakotas—and he also defined his stance, which was the position of a Republican affiliated with no "ring" or "clique." After the letters had been sent, he targeted key assemblymen for personal follow-up visits. He made it a point not to call exclusively on men who lived in Albany, New York, and the other big cities, the men who were easy and convenient to visit, but instead singled out representatives who lived in the smallest, most remote rural hamlets of the Empire State. Calling on them, Roosevelt knew, required a train ride, followed by a buggy ride, and—often—a long hike. Roosevelt also knew that the only person more aware than he of the required effort was the man on whom he was calling.

> **Personal contact has always** been valuable in business. Today, however, when email, conference calls, virtual whiteboard meeting technology, and instant messaging have for many rendered personal visits obsolete, real-life face time, though technologically "unnecessary," is more precious and powerful than ever. Take the time, the effort, and the expense to call on a business contact personally, and you convey the message of that person's great value to you. Exert yourself, and you find that you command the remarkable force of real life.

■

*Lesson 95*
## Make Good Use of Defeat

> "The fact that I had fought hard and efficiently . . . and that I had made the fight single-handed, with no machine back of me, assured my standing as floor leader. My defeat in the end materially strengthened my position, and enabled me to accomplish far more than I could have accomplished as Speaker."
>
> ~ *An Autobiography*, 1913

In 1883, second-term New York State assemblyman Theodore Roosevelt made an audacious bid for election as speaker. He deliberately ran as his own man, without the support of the party machine, in the hope that his fellow Republicans would welcome a speaker who was beholden to no group, sect, clique, special interest, boss, or other individual. He mounted an intensely personal campaign, sending letters to all members of the party and following up many of them with a face-to-face visit, often traveling to the most remote rural corners of the state to pay a call. It was a campaign as brilliant as it was exhausting, but, in the end, Roosevelt lost to Titus Sheard, a regular party man.

In the immediate aftermath of his defeat, Roosevelt was clearly shaken. To intimates, he confessed "chagrin"—a powerful expression of disappointment from a man so habitually positive in outlook and demeanor—and friends reported that the young "dude" had been transformed into a weary and aged being.

This transformation did not last long.

As Roosevelt explained years later in his autobiography, he soon realized—or at least decided—that defeat was not only as valuable as victory would have been, but actually even more valuable, enabling him "to accomplish far more than I could have accomplished as Speaker." He had fought the good fight, and that did not go unappreciated. He believed that his position in the assembly had been strengthened by the effort he made. Nor was this the self-delusion of a loser. Speaker Sheard proved generous to his opponent when it came to doling out committee appointments, giving Roosevelt his choice of plums. In short order, at his request, Roosevelt was named to the Militia, Banks, and Cities committees, even gaining appointment as chairman of the latter. From this position, he wielded much influence as a reformer. It proved to be his ticket to statewide and even national prominence.

**"You are not beaten,"** World War II general George S. Patton Jr. advised young officers, "until you admit defeat. Hence, don't." Roosevelt was disappointed by his loss of the New York Assembly speakership, but, after a brief emotional struggle, he transformed the defeat into an opportunity to display to others just what a determined fighter he was and how far he could take himself, "single-handed, with no machine back of me."

In the balancing of means and ends, there is a compelling temptation to give almost all the weight to ends. This is a mistake, because it discards and wastes the means, which can also be a very valuable commodity. Tangible effort has an effect, even if the ultimate result fails to go your way. Make your process strong, then make good use of that process. Fight, wit, will, perseverance, efficiency, and character are means. Put them on display. Do not let "failure" or "defeat" erase them.

■

### Lesson 96
## To Stand Tall Is Best, but to Bend Is Better Than to Break

> "Now and then one can stand uncompromisingly for a naked principle and force people up to it. This is always the attractive course; but in certain great crises it may be the wrong course."
> ~Remarks in *The Century*, June 1900

To think of Theodore Roosevelt is to picture an icon of principle, a defiant leader prepared to fight for an absolute ideal. This was, to be sure, an important aspect of TR's political philosophy and personal character, and it was an aspect he himself considered most "attractive." Nevertheless, Roosevelt was first and foremost a politician, not an idealist. "No student of American history needs to be reminded," he wrote in *The Century* in 1900, "that the Constitution itself is a bundle of compromises." John Martin Blum, in *The Republican Roosevelt* (1954), quoted TR as calling compromises "great temptations" yet also conceding that "public men" are "always obliged to compromise in order to do anything." Indeed, as Roosevelt himself observed in his own popular biography of that most unbending of political leaders, Oliver Cromwell, "Self-governing freemen must have the power to accept necessary compromises, to make necessary concessions, each sacrificing somewhat of prejudice, and even of principle, and every group must show the necessary subordination of its particular interests [to the interests] of the community as a whole."

Compromise was a necessity as well as a convenient tool. It was often the only means of advancement, of getting things accomplished. Without question, it was always preferable to stand on principle; however, this was not always possible—and, sometimes, it was even the "wrong course," no matter how "attractive." Still, one should never abandon one's moral compass in navigating the sometimes treacherous waters of compromise. "A compromise which results in a half-step toward evil is all wrong." While Roosevelt might compromise an end—getting less than he wanted or giving more than he wanted in order to get something important that he wanted—he would not compromise the morality of means in order to achieve any end.

> **Absolute adherence to principle** always seems the most desirable course, but if adherence to what you hold as the best requires sacrificing the good while at the same time failing to attain the best, it is the *wrong* course. The *right* course is the best course available under the circumstances. It is the course that compromises principle without sacrificing principle. Above all, it is *a* course: movement in a productive direction.
>
> Deeds, imperfect though they may be, are dynamic: productive. Ideology, as perfect as it may be, is static: sterile.

■

*Lesson 97*
# Beware the Timidity of Ambition

"Never, never, you must never . . . remind a man at work on a
political job that he may be President. It almost always kills him
politically. He loses his nerve; he can't do his work; he gives up
the very traits that are making him a possibility."
~ To his friends Lincoln Steffens and Jacob Riis, November 1896

Theodore Roosevelt's bravura performance as the dauntless and
tireless president of the New York Police Board set local and even
national politicos talking him up as prime presidential timber.
When the journalists Lincoln Steffens and Jacob Riis cheerfully
informed Roosevelt of what they were hearing about him, the
commissioner responded not with delight but recoiled in horror. If
you tell a man that he is in line for the biggest job in the world, his
first impulse is to retreat into a timidity that will make him unfit for
*any* political office, let alone the presidency.

**"Ambition" and "timidity"** would seem mutually exclusive
qualities, but, as TR understood, they may actually go hand in
hand. The greater the prize you covet, the more anxious you
may be to hang on to what gains you have already made, lest
you stumble and lose what you hold. But the fact is that you
cannot build a successful leadership career on a mountain of
*don'ts*. Advance requires *doing*. To avoid action is to stand still
and, most probably, to be swept back. Leaders rise by poking
their heads above those of the crowd. It's the only way to get
yourself noticed, even though it surely puts your neck at risk.

## Lesson 98
# Call Yourself an American

"Don't let them bluff you out of the use of the word 'American.'
[Call] yourself the American Ambassador and [use] the word
American instead of the United States."
~Letter to John Hay, U.S. ambassador to the court
of St. James's, London, June 7, 1897

Citizens of the United States have long called themselves *Americans* and their nation *America*. Canadians and Mexicans have sometimes objected to this linguistic usurpation, but to no avail. Teddy Roosevelt harbored no guilt over laying claim to a continent shared not only with Canada and Mexico (combined population today, 146,000,000), but with the seven nations of Central America (41,739,000 people) and some thirty Caribbean countries and dependencies (about 40,800,000 people). On the contrary, he advised the ambassador to the United Kingdom to resist all attempts by anyone to "bluff" him out of using *American* in preference to the far more politically accurate *United States*, even in official reference to his own office.

Was this insistence sheer arrogance and obstinacy? More darkly (in the view of some), was this a symptom of TR's unapologetic imperialism, his desire to build an American empire?

Perhaps. But as motives for replacing *United States* with *America* and *American*, these collectively take a distant second place to TR's abiding desire to create an enduring national identity for himself and his people. For him, *United States* was a legal and political designation, nothing less but nothing more. It was insufficient in scope and depth to both describe and evoke the historical, emotional, intellectual, spiritual, and visceral dimensions of the American identity. Unlike the designation *United States*, the concept of *America* embodied nationhood in the fullest possible sense, encompassing elements of civilization, shared ideals, common destiny, and what can only be described as a survival of tribalism in the modern world. *United States* might be a politically significant label, but *America* packed a potency beyond politics—or, rather, a power that both expanded and deepened the people's understanding of politics, of what it means to be a citizen, an *American* citizen.

Theodore Roosevelt's own bigger-than-life life was a celebration of the individual, and yet his ultimate philosophy of political leadership culminated in the "New Nationalism" that was the keynote of his 1912 third-party campaign for the presidency. It was the simultaneous exaltation of the individual and the subordination of the individual to the nation. It was a practical expression of the national motto, *E pluribus unum*: Of many, one. But that one had to be great enough—big enough, all-encompassing enough—to accommodate the many as *individuals*. For Roosevelt, *America* rather than the *United States* was big enough.

**Define your enterprise in** ways that reveal it as worthy of all-out collaboration. This means defining an organization greater than the sum of its parts: a collective endeavor that elevates each of the individuals who contribute to it.

■

### Lesson 99
## Leader or Extremist?

"While extremists are sometimes men who are in advance of their age, more often they are men who are not in advance at all, but simply to one side or the other of a great movement, or even lagging behind it, or trying to pilot it in the wrong direction."

~Oliver Cromwell

There was never any shortage of people ready to label Theodore Roosevelt an extremist. He understood the label as more often appropriate for those at the political fringes—who, if followed, would lead in the wrong direction—than for those truly "in advance of their age." Thus Roosevelt distrusted extremism and believed that, far from being an extremist himself, he was a genuine leader: more in step with his age than in advance of it, but in the vanguard nevertheless. If making himself conspicuous in this position caused some to confound him with a denizen of the fringe, the error was theirs, not his.

Of course, the real question was how anyone, TR included, might prove himself to be a leader as opposed to an extremist. Roosevelt never answered this directly, but his whole life nevertheless points to his answer. A leader *knows* he is right. To the obvious objection that an extremist also claims to *know* that he is right, Roosevelt would simply have answered, *Yes, but he would be mistaken.*

**You will search in** vain for an objective test of whether you are a leader or a mere extremist. Results are a good indication. But by the time you have produced measurable results, you and your enterprise may have crashed. There is no choice but to rely on your own convictions as informed by your sense of just where you have positioned yourself in your organization. You need to feel yourself at the front, looking forward, but not so far out in front that you can no longer feel the collective breath of the enterprise on the back of your neck.

■

## *Lesson 100*
## Carry That Big Stick

> "There is a homely adage which runs, 'Speak softly and carry a big stick; you will go far.' If the American nation will speak softly and yet build and keep at a pitch of the highest training a thoroughly efficient navy, the Monroe Doctrine will go far."
>
> ~Speech, Minnesota State Fair, September 2, 1901

It's the one thing everybody knows—or thinks they know—about Teddy Roosevelt: *He's the president who believed in speaking softly but carrying a big stick.*

Since the turn of the century, Americans, a people who have always liked headlines, have taken this expression to be the sum and substance of the Roosevelt foreign policy, which they have frequently labeled "belligerent" and "bellicose." The facts of the Roosevelt administration argue otherwise. The Roosevelt presidency years were ones of peace and prosperity, and the president himself was awarded a Nobel Peace Prize for his role in ending the extraordinarily bloody Russo-Japanese War of 1905.

At the hour that Roosevelt made reference to the "homely adage" (many believe it is a West African proverb) about soft speech and the big stick, he was still vice president of the United States. In just four days, President McKinley would be mortally wounded by an assassin's bullets, but no one knew that on September 2, when the vice president was doing the job vice presidents did back then: making a speech to an audience on an occasion that didn't quite rate a presidential visit and address. Just as he could not know that he was about to step into the White House, so he did not know—let alone intend—that the "big stick" would become his diplomatic trademark.

In context, his speech in September 1901 was fairly narrow in its intended application. It was meant as nothing more than a justification for spending a great deal of money to build up a large United States Navy. A few years earlier, in a June 2, 1897, speech at

Newport, Rhode Island, he had put it this way: "Diplomacy is utterly useless where there is no force behind it." A strong American navy would be the "force" necessary to back a vigorous American diplomacy. Commanding such a force, the United States would never have to bellow through its diplomats but, on the contrary, could speak softly and reasonably through them. As Roosevelt saw it, developing a formidable force—a strong army and an even stronger navy (for the United States lay between two great oceans)— was not a gesture of war, but a means of keeping the peace, albeit on terms favorable to America. Only a fool, after all, would attack a man who carries a big stick.

**Only careless talkers use** the word *credibility* as a synonym for *truthfulness*. The fuller meaning of *credibility* is that the words a credible person utters are not hollow but, rather, convey the solid substance of action. Commanding a large navy did not oblige Theodore Roosevelt to go to war, but it made credible to all other nations the dreadful prospect of war should they cross the interests of the United States. Acquiring the means of action does not oblige you to exercise force, but it does bolster your words with the very real prospect of decisive action to follow.

Make no hollow threats (speak softly), but do ensure that others understand the full extent of the resources and authority you wield. If they do, you will never have to raise your voice to deliver a threat. Those to whom you speak softly will make all the necessary connections for themselves. That is credibility.

■

*Lesson 101*
## Exercise Grace

"I want your friendship."

~ To Senator Mark Hanna, September 14, 1901

Mark Hanna, United States senator from Ohio, was, like Theodore Roosevelt, a Republican. With that, any similarity between the two men ended.

Hanna was an organization man, a kingmaker in the party, an industrialist whose allegiance was to capital rather than to labor and to a status quo that was prosperous—at least for men of own his social and economic station. He feared Roosevelt as a wild-eyed reformer, even something of a socialist, and when he heard that President McKinley had died of his wounds, he was beside himself and cried out: "Now look—that damned cowboy is President of the United States!"

Hanna paid a call on the new president shortly after he had taken the oath of office on the afternoon of September 14, 1901. Roosevelt was keenly aware that Hanna had worshiped McKinley and was crushed by his death, and he was equally cognizant that Hanna bore him no love whatsoever. Yet when he saw the old senator's carriage drive up and the nearly broken man make his way unsteadily to the porch, weakly relying on a cane, President Roosevelt quickly descended the porch steps, his arm outstretched in greeting. Not for him to wait in expectation of Hanna's homage.

For his part, Mark Hanna responded to the gesture of respect.

"Mr. President," he began, "I wish you success and prosperous administration. Sir, I trust that you will command me if I can be of service."

Roosevelt uttered no such "command."

"I want your friendship," he said as he helped the tired, shaken old man up the steps.

**Business manipulates money,** merchandise, and ideas, but most of all, business advances or falls as a result of contact between people. Gestures of humanity, understanding, empathy, kindness, integrity, gratitude, and respect—gestures of grace—can work powerfully and even unexpectedly. Practice them.

■

### Lesson 102
## Say the Right Thing

"And in this hour of deep and terrible national bereavement I wish to state that it shall be my aim to continue absolutely unbroken the policy of President McKinley."

~Remark before taking the oath of office to succeed President William McKinley, September 14, 1901

Theodore Roosevelt succeeded to the presidency on the death, by assassination, of William McKinley. He would immediately prove a far stronger, more dynamic, and more innovative president that his predecessor, yet he followed the advice of Elihu Root, McKinley's secretary of war, that he (in Root's words) "declare his intention to continue unbroken the policy of President McKinley." In fact, he repeated this phrase almost word for word.

It was not insincere. It was not a lie. It was just a partial truth. More important, the new president understood that, with the nation in shock from the violent death of a president who had presided over victory in the Spanish-American War and who governed a country enjoying prosperity and peace, change was the last thing people wanted to hear about. Theodore Roosevelt typically spoke his mind and heart. Right now, however, he decided to say the right thing, the thing the nation needed to hear.

[ 171 ]

His pledge was received with great favor, not only in the United States, but throughout the world. But when it came time to take the actual oath of office, TR asserted himself with a degree of drama immediately demonstrating that he would be no one's follower. Witnesses described his stance as that of a marble statue. He did not merely repeat the words of the oath of office administered by a local federal judge, but articulated them loudly and precisely—then even embellished the constitutional oath by ending his recitation with the sentence, "And thus I swear." In this way, he punctuated his promise to continue unbroken the policies of his predecessor with a dramatic performance that revealed him as his own, very strong, man.

> **As a leader, you** are obligated both to tell the truth and to speak the words your organization needs to hear. Nevertheless, at times, without lying, you must also say the "right" thing—not necessarily what the enterprise *needs* to hear, but what it *wants* to hear.

■

*Lesson 103*
## Lead Everyone

"The great corporations which we have grown to speak of rather loosely as trusts are the creatures of the State, and the State not only has the right to control them, but it is in duty bound to control them wherever the need of such control is shown . . . . The immediate necessity in dealing with trusts is to place them under the real, not the nominal, control of some sovereign to which, as its creatures, the trusts shall owe allegiance, and in whose courts the sovereign's orders may be enforced . . . . In my judgment this sovereign must be the national government."

~Speech, Providence, Rhode Island, August 23, 1902

Grade-school history remembers President Theodore Roosevelt as the "trust buster," the chief executive who crusaded against the unregulated monopolies that threatened to destroy marketplace competition and hold consumers of any number of essential goods and services hostage. The speech the president made at Providence, Rhode Island, on August 23, 1902, is generally considered to be his first public statement concerning the federal government's right and responsibility to regulate the trusts, and the passage quoted at the top of this lesson is among TR's most succinct expressions of the role government should take in regulating commerce.

Doubtless many who read these few sentences today will be shocked by their apparent radicalism. Ever since the two terms of Ronald Reagan, the trend in the United States has been toward deregulation and the general withdrawal of the federal government from private enterprise. In Roosevelt's own day, there were many powerful business and financial interests that objected to his stance on trusts. And yet Teddy Roosevelt was—and remains to this conservative day—one of the nation's most popular leaders.

How did he do it?

Some have tried to explain his enduring popularity strictly in terms of the appeal of his colorful, bigger-than-life personality and presence. There is some validity to this explanation as far as it goes, but it does not go far enough. The fact is that while Roosevelt took many bold stands and proposed a number of sweeping and fundamental changes in the role of the federal government, he never forgot that his constituency was the people of the United States of America. He was everyone's president. He was not the president of big business. He was not the president of labor. He was not the rich man's president. He was not the president of the downtrodden. He was the president of the United States.

As some will read it, the passage quoted at the top of this lesson paints TR as pro–federal government and anti–big business. Even the most objective reader must conclude that the president's sympathies lay with the people rather than the corporate interests.

But these ninety-nine words are not all that Theodore Roosevelt said to this audience that day. He led up to his "trust busting" passage by observing that—

> We are passing through a period of great commercial prosperity, and such a period is as sure as adversity itself to bring mutterings of discontent. At a time when most men prosper somewhat some men always prosper greatly; and it is as true now as when the tower of Siloam fell upon all alike, that good fortune does not come solely to the just, nor bad fortune solely to the unjust. When the weather is good for crops it is also good for weeds.

Thus Roosevelt began by addressing everyone of every social order, explaining that while prosperity was general, it most assuredly was not evenly distributed. Many prospered "somewhat" while some prospered "greatly." If this was an injustice—and the president does not concede that it was—then it was an injustice that has endured as long as human civilization itself, even in the days of Jesus, when the ancient tower of Siloam, in Jerusalem, fell upon rich and poor, good and wicked alike, indiscriminately killing eighteen people, according to the Gospel of Luke. Prosperity benefits all and not necessarily in proportion to each person's "just" desserts.

So the president begins by defining the limits of his power and of the power of government to mete out absolute justice. And so he begins, in addressing everyone, by effectively defining himself as everyone's leader. If his powers are limited, they are limited over everyone. That is the way civilized social life is and the way it has always been.

The president goes on to explain that, in civilized societies— "Where men are gathered together in great masses it inevitably results that they must work far more largely through combinations than when they live scattered and remote from one another." This being the case, "present-day conditions" make it "necessary to have corporations in the business world." Thus Roosevelt shows that he is president of corporate America. Then he goes on to explain that it is also *just* as necessary "to have organizations, unions, among wage workers." Now he shows himself to be president of labor. This balanced approach was typical of a Roosevelt speech.

Presented with apparently incompatible extremes in conflict—in this case, the trusts versus labor—TR always looked for a way to navigate between them. They may conflict, corporations and labor unions, but they are both necessary. He goes on to describe the conflict yet more sharply; however, even as he does this, he makes the middle course yet clearer and more compelling: "Every man of power, by the very fact of that power, is capable of doing damage to his neighbors." There is one side. But the sentence does not end here. Instead, it balances on a "but" that acts as a kind of rhetorical fulcrum: "but we cannot afford to discourage the development of such men merely because it is possible they may use their power for wrong ends." In fact, the president warns, "the greatest harm done by vast wealth "is not done by the people of wealth themselves, but by "we of moderate means," who harm ourselves "when we let the vices of envy and hatred enter deep in our own natures."

In this careful manner, Roosevelt leads up to his "radical" stance on trusts. He defines himself as everyone's president. Having done this, he goes on to define two sources of social harm: One is the unchecked power of great wealth. The other is class warfare, the "vice of envy and hatred" in the hearts of "we of moderate means." Thus his solution, federal regulation of corporations ("creatures of the State" in that they operate by legal authority of the state), is proposed as a solution to *both* sources of social harm. The regulation of trusts is not to punish wealth nor to reward those of moderate means, but to preserve and defend the United States, which includes everyone, regardless of income and station.

**Invited to mount the** sharp horns of a dilemma, politely decline to take the proffered seat. Theodore Roosevelt entered the White House in a time of deep cultural and economic division in the United States. His answer to this division was not to favor one side or the other, or somehow to force unity upon the nation, but rather to ensure that he presented himself as the nation's president—everyone's leader.

Resolve to lead your organization. Make all of your decisions, including those relating to apparently conflicting interests and opposing points of view, from the perspective of the collective singularity of the entire enterprise. If you must take sides, take sides on behalf of everyone. It can be done. It must be done.

■

*Lesson 104*
## Balance Is Not a Synonym for Status Quo

"Arrogance, suspicion, brutal envy of the well-to-do, brutal indifference toward those who are not well-to-do, the hard refusal to consider the rights of others, the foolish refusal to consider the limits of beneficent action, the base appeal to the spirit of selfish greed, whether it take the form of plunder of the fortunate or of oppression of the unfortunate—from these and from all kindred vices this Nation must be kept free if it is to remain in its present position in the forefront of the peoples of mankind."

~ Address to the Chamber of Commerce of
New York City, November 11, 1902

The general prosperity of the United States during the administration of Theodore Roosevelt belied deep and deepening divisions among the people. No one was more aware of these than the president himself. One of his best friends, Jacob Riis, a man he had come to know well when he served as president of the Police Board of New York City early in his political career, had written an eye-opening documentary covering New York slum life, whose very title, *How the Other Half Lives*, expressed the essence of the national divide.

Schoolbook history correctly notes that Roosevelt was profoundly moved by *How the Other Half Lives* and similar documents exposing economically based injustice in America. Inspired, President Roosevelt championed enlightened welfare legislation, consumer protection laws, passage of a Pure Food and Drug Act creating the FDA, the strict regulation of trusts and banking, and related reforms. The impression we are left with is that President Roosevelt was the tireless advocate of "the other half."

And so he was. But that was only half the story and half of his approach to leadership. Theodore Roosevelt would never be content with serving as president of half the people.

The speech he gave to the Chamber of Commerce in New York in 1902 is vintage TR. The structure of each sentence is as balanced as the content. What he condemns as the "Arrogance, suspicion, brutal envy of the well-to-do" is balanced by what he condemns equally as "the brutal indifference toward those who are not well-to-do." The adjective *brutal* is applied to both cases, and the noun "well-to-do" is perfectly opposed by its negation in the phrase "those who are not well-to-do." The "hard refusal to consider the rights of others" is exactly balanced against "the foolish refusal to consider the limits of beneficent action." Neglect is "hard," yet a belief that the government can fix everything is "foolish." As for demagoguery, it is evil whatever side practices it: "the base appeal to the spirit of selfish greed, whether it take the form of plunder of the fortunate or of oppression of the unfortunate." *Plunder* is precisely counterpointed by *oppression, the fortunate by the unfortunate*.

Through precisely balanced syntax and content, Roosevelt sought to present himself as the leader not of this or that faction, not of this or the other half of America, but of the entire nation. As he saw it, this exquisite balancing act was absolutely essential, yet it was not without risk. For in trying to serve both sides, there is risk of satisfying neither. Moreover, *balance* is readily confused with preserving the *status quo*. Roosevelt maneuvered around this by refusing to attack people–either the "fortunate" or the "unfortunate"–and instead attacked the "vices" he had enumerated as afflicting both sides and all extremes. Effective change could not come at the total expense of one side or the other, but through a change in common sentiment, motives, and values. The only way to change the status quo for the better without punishing half the nation was to be resolute in leading all of the nation.

**You can achieve productive** growth and change only if you lead your enterprise in ways that do not pit person against person, interest against interest, and faction against faction. Identify issues that represent problems, values, or benefits for the organization as a whole. Through balanced policies and communication, direct the group's energy toward these, the common stake in which all partake.

■

*Lesson 105*
## Refuse to Be a Victim

"If it had been I who had been shot, he wouldn't have got away so easily. . . . I'd have guzzled him first."
~Remark shortly after receiving news of
President McKinley's death, quoted in
Edmund Morris, *Theodore Rex*, 2001

It is obvious, easy, and not necessarily incorrect to chalk up Roosevelt's bellicose response to a hypothetical assassination attempt to some combination of impotent outrage and bravado, but, whatever else motivated the remark, it also sprang from an impulse natural to Roosevelt both as the kind of man he was and as a political animal. He refused to wear an identity he did not himself invent. It did not matter whether it was a newspaperman trying to slap an unwanted label on him with a story or an assassin attempting to brand him as a victim by drilling him with lead. He would tolerate neither attempt at transformation imposed from the outside.

To be sure, Roosevelt accepted the possibility of assassination. What happened to McKinley—and to James Garfield and Abraham Lincoln before him—was irrefutable proof of that possibility. For that matter, Roosevelt himself would be wounded by a gunman on October 14, 1912, during his third-party presidential campaign. He did not deny or even defy the possibility of assassination. However, in vowing that he would have "guzzled" his assailant (by which he seems to have meant slugged) before he could get away, Roosevelt did refuse to be branded a victim. Gunned down, he would nevertheless have remained an aggressor, exercising in this his right and determination to assert himself in creating and preserving his own identity.

**If you fail to** brand yourself, others will brand you. Decide who you are, who you want to be, and how you want others to see you. Take every opportunity to present yourself in the context of the identity you design. Defend against all outside efforts to rebrand you. To allow your image to be remolded by other hands is to surrender leadership.

*Lesson 106*
## Give Up Politics, Take Up Leadership

"It is a dreadful misfortune for a man to grow to feel that his whole livelihood and whole happiness depend upon his staying in office."

*~ An Autobiography,* 1913

Theodore Roosevelt loved politics. His first national political campaign was as William McKinley's running mate, a position from which he did far more campaigning far more effectively than the presidential candidate himself. From the get-go, he revealed himself to be an irrepressible political animal.

This said, Roosevelt distrusted politics his whole life. Not only did he grow to resent the hold it had on him—the feeling that everything depended on staying in office—but he understood all too keenly that the motives of politics did not always coincide with those of leadership. When he declared before the New York State Assembly in March 1883, "I would rather go out of politics having the feeling that I had done what was right than stay in with the approval of all men, knowing in my heart that I had acted as I ought not to," he opted for leadership instead of politics.

The mark of a committed politician is the willingness to yield leadership to those who put him (and keep him) in office. The mark of a committed leader is the willingness to leave politics altogether, even if this means stepping down from leadership forever. This is the bargain Roosevelt struck and stuck to.

**A politician follows at** least as much as she leads and, the more she wants to cling to office, the more she will be tempted to follow *more* than she leads. The leader, in contrast to the politician, voluntarily yields no prerogative or responsibility and risks her place at the head of the column every single day. You must decide—now—which you want to be: politician or leader.

*Lesson 107*
## Make It Either/Or

"WE WANT PERDICARIS ALIVE OR RAISULI DEAD."
~Secretary of State John Hay's cabled instructions to
Samuel R. Gummeré, U.S. consul to Morocco, June 1904

Ion Perdicaris was the son of Gregory Perdicaris, a Greek immigrant to the United States who, after marrying into a prosperous South Carolina family, served for a time as the U.S. consul to Greece and then settled in Trenton, New Jersey, where he amassed a fortune as a founder of the Trenton Gas Company. Gregory lavished his indulgence on young Ion, who lived a playboy life until 1862, when the Confederate government made moves to confiscate the family's property in South Carolina. Ion sought to prevent this by returning to Greece, there renouncing his U.S. citizenship and invoking international law, as a Greek national, to block confiscation.

Ion remained abroad, settled in Tangier, and built an extravagant mansion he called the Place of Nightingales, in which he led a more than mildly scandalous life with Ellen Varley, the erstwhile wife of C. F. Varley, a world-famous telegraph engineer. After the Varleys finally divorced in 1873, Ellen and Ion Perdicaris continued to live in the Place of Nightingales with her four children by C. F. Varley.

On May 18, 1904, revolutionary bandits under Mulai Ahmed er Raisuli (or Raisuni), considered by many the rightful heir to the Moroccan throne, abducted Ion Perdicaris and one of Ellen's sons, Cromwell, from the Place of Nightingales. In return for the release of the pair, Raisuli demanded from the Moroccan sultan Abdelaziz a $70,000 ransom as well as control of two of Morocco's wealthiest districts. President Roosevelt, however, was not content to leave the fate of someone he believed (mistakenly, as it turned out) to be an American citizen in the hands of a foreign "brigand" and a Moroccan potentate. He therefore ordered U.S. admiral French Ensor Chadwick to lead seven warships, with fully equipped

U.S. Marine companies on board, to Morocco. Through Secretary of State John Hay, he cabled to U.S. consul Samuel R. Gummeré an ultimatum to be delivered to the sultan and instructions for backing it up. "WE WANT PERDICARIS ALIVE OR RAISULI DEAD," the message began starkly.

FURTHER THAN THIS WE DESIRE LEAST POSSIBLE COMPLICATIONS WITH MOROCCO OR OTHER POWERS. YOU WILL NOT ARRANGE FOR LANDING MARINES OR SEIZING CUSTOM HOUSE WITHOUT SPECIFIC DIRECTIONS FROM THE [STATE] DEPARTMENT.

The president had no wish to create an international incident, especially after it was discovered, early in June, that Pedicaris had, in fact, renounced his U.S. citizenship. Yet the world believed he was an American, and President Roosevelt did not want to split legal hairs. If the world thought Ion Perdicaris was a U.S. national, he, the U.S. president, would protect him.

Roosevelt did try to hedge his bet by soliciting the cooperation of Great Britain and France in a joint armed rescue mission, but was turned down—publicly. Privately, the French and the English responded by pressuring Sultan Abdelaziz to accede to all of Raisuli's demands. The sultan yielded on June 21, whereupon, with the president's blessing, Hay released the first line of the cable—"WE WANT PERDICARIS ALIVE OR RAISULI DEAD"—to the Republican National Convention.

Some delegates protested Roosevelt's bellicosity. Some thought that releasing the cable to the convention and to the press was an outrage. But most were thrilled and became wildly enthusiastic to nominate Theodore Roosevelt as the Republican candidate for the presidency in his own right. "Our people like courage," a Kansas delegate declared. "We'll stand for anything those men [meaning

Hay and Roosevelt] do." The nomination, when it came, was unanimous. As for Ion Perdicaris, he and Cromwell Varley were released unharmed.

> **Poker players know that** the bluff is an important weapon in the game's arsenal; away from the poker table, however, empty threats are never a good idea. At times, however, there is nothing more effective than an either/or proposition, an ultimatum persuasively backed by the manifest reality of tangible consequences.

■

## Lesson 108
## Broadcast Your Destiny

"Must be President some day. A man you can't cajole, can't frighten, can't buy."

~Bram Stoker, *Reminiscences of Sir Henry Irving*, 1906

The Irish novelist Bram Stoker first encountered Theodore Roosevelt in New York in 1895. At the time, Roosevelt was making a sensation as the city's dynamic and incorruptible president of the Police Board, and Stoker was two years away from publication of the work that would make him world famous, *Dracula.*

Stoker's prediction about Roosevelt–"Must be President some day"–was not unique. A number of perceptive men and women saw precisely this prospect at some time during every stage of Roosevelt's early career: in the New York State Assembly, in the Dakota Badlands, and on the mean streets of New York City. Whereas most of the others cited Roosevelt's energy and charisma, Stoker, however, was more incisive. The presidential qualities he saw in Roosevelt were not attributes of a powerful personal aura, but the tangible products of his actions. His words and deeds as New York's top cop showed him to be what Stoker called him: "a man you can't cajole, can't frighten, can't buy."

> **If you want to** persuade people that you are destined to do great things, start doing great things. Broadcast your destiny through action. Begin the program today. You haven't a moment to lose.

■

## Lesson 109
## Fair Should Feel Right

"Our constant aim is to do justice to every man, and to treat each man as by his own actions he shows that he deserves to be treated."

~Speech, Oyster Bay, New York, August 18, 1906

Roosevelt made an early name for himself in politics as a crusader against the old "spoils system" of political patronage whereby lucrative government appointments were handed out not on the basis of *what* the appointee knew but on *who* he knew. Jobs were political favors granted or political debts repaid. Merit typically did not even enter into the transaction. Like other Progressives, Roosevelt sought to lift the administration of government from the status of spoils divvied up to merit recruited, recognized, and rewarded. Democracy, he believed, could not survive as a patronage bazaar but had to become a true meritocracy.

Understandably, the political establishment of Roosevelt's day objected to his reforms. Just as understandably, however, the reforms met with widespread popular approval. Professional politicians might be unhappy, but to the people, the idea of meritocracy simply felt right. It was part and parcel of the commonsense definition of justice Roosevelt put into words in a speech from his Oyster Bay porch on August 18, 1906: the doctrine of treating "each man as by his own actions he shows that he deserves to be treated." There was no abstract theory involved. There was no high-flown idealism, either. It was simply the application of a principle whose rightness everyone naturally feels. It is the elementary, even childlike, principle of merit and just desserts.

> **Leadership is not conferred** by job title. Leadership is not handed down. Leadership is handed up, earned every day from those you lead. Fail to earn it, and your job title may or may not remain unchanged, but you will certainly cease to be a leader. Every member of your organization must feel the fairness of the decisions that affect them. Absent this feeling, they will soon stop handing up to you your right to lead. Make fairness central to your leadership and make the basis of your justice obvious beyond all doubt and dispute. What's fair should unmistakably feel right.

■

*Lesson 110*
## Go Ahead, Rattle That Saber

"The most important service that I rendered to peace was the voyage of the battle fleet round the world."

~ *An Autobiography*, 1913

On December 16, 1907, pursuant to orders from the president, sixteen recently built battleships of the U.S. Navy's Atlantic Fleet set out on a circumnavigation, which would be completed on February 22, 1909. The hulls of the ships had been painted a dazzling white, which was the livery of the peacetime navy, and thus the world greeted the "Great White Fleet" of the United

States. Manned by 14,000 sailors, the vessels traversed 43,000 nautical miles and touched twenty major ports on six continents. As TR explained in his 1913 autobiography, his intention in sending out the fleet had been to ensure that it was "clearly understood by our own people especially, but also by other peoples, that the Pacific was as much our home waters as the Atlantic."

Although the Great White Fleet was universally greeted with friendly enthusiasm, there were and have always been critics who called the expedition an exercise in saber rattling. The president would not have denied this. Yet, as he observed, his intention was far from belligerent. By exhibiting the might of the United States—most specifically its ability and willingness to project a mighty force anywhere in the world—President Roosevelt not only asserted America's international interests and rights, but promoted peace by discouraging aggression against the United States. The voyage of the Great White Fleet was the most spectacular demonstration of what historians have called Roosevelt's "big stick" diplomacy. He made no threats—on the contrary, the nation's diplomats spoke softly—but he did not hesitate to exhibit the big stick that was the national capacity for force.

Remarkably, sixteen battleships, bristling with firepower, delivered a message far more subtle than may be at first apparent. The world's diplomats and military leaders understood that white was the color scheme of the *peacetime* United States Navy. The ships did not travel in gray battle dress. Moreover, as new vessels, they were not simply weapons of war, but gleaming steel evidence of the industrial and economic prowess of the nation that built them. While the fleet's voyage was a warning, it was even more an offer of friendship—of profitable commerce and trade—from a powerful friend. It was in this carefully compounded mixture of messages that the potent genius of this particular manifestation of "big stick" diplomacy lay.

**A display of force** need not be an act of aggression. Craft your messages with care, deliver them with panache, make no empty threats, and balance warning with invitation.

■

*Lesson 111*
## Make Idealism Realism

"It is time for us now as a Nation to exercise the same reasonable foresight in dealing with our great natural resources that would be shown by any prudent man in conserving and wisely using the property which contains the assurance of well-being for himself and his children."

~ Opening address to the Conference on the Conservation of Natural Resources, White House, May 13, 1908

To many Americans at the turn of the twentieth century (as even now, at the turn of the twenty-first), the cause of national conservation seemed an ideological ideal in mortal conflict with the hallowed realities of private property, private enterprise, and the constitutional right to exploit whatever resources one was rich and powerful enough to purchase, own, and control. Combative by nature, President Roosevelt might easily have fallen into the trap of this opposition by simply and forcefully insisting that the collective welfare of the nation trumped the so-called right of individual use and exploitation. Indeed, he certainly felt that it did. But, as a skilled political leader and communicator, he knew better than to exacerbate a conflict that already existed. Instead of taking a combative stance, he formulated a vision that aimed to make the ideal real and the apparently lofty down to earth. He reduced a national vision to a matter of individual common sense.

He did this by rendering his national vision in terms of "any prudent man." He did not present the creation of a national policy of conservation as an altruistic sacrifice of certain rights of private property in the name of the collective good, but as a simple commonsense extension of what anyone does for "the assurance of well-being for himself and his children."

**Here is the heart** of TR's genius for selling his vision to the "common man:" He powerfully and simply communicated to everyone the stake that they, individually, held in the collective future of the nation. Inspiration and motivation need not take place on the stratospheric level of lofty idealism. Translate your imperatives into common sense, and you will make common cause. The homelier you make your ideals appear, the more obviously desirable and necessary they will seem. Your job, as a leader, is not to motivate your organization, but to move its individual members.

■

*Lesson 112*
## Accept the Limits of Objectivity

"Every time they [judges] interpret contract, property, invested rights . . . they necessarily enact into law parts of a system of social philosophy. . . . The decisions of the courts on economic and social questions depend on their economic and social philosophy."
~Annual message to Congress, December 8, 1908

Theodore Roosevelt understood the ideal of blind justice, but he did not make the mistake of blindly believing in it. Although he presided over what John Adams had called a "government of laws, not men," he accepted the unavoidable truth that laws are created, interpreted, and administered by people. He further accepted the equally unavoidable truth that no human heart or human mind is capable of total objectivity. All judgment, even the noblest and best informed, depended on the "philosophy" of the person who made the judgment. Nowhere was this more evident than in decisions "on economic and social questions," which depended on the "economic and social philosophy" of the judge.

Roosevelt did not decry or condemn these truths. They were, after all, integral to human nature and human society, and so he accepted them. Nevertheless, he did insist that they be acknowledged, recognized, and managed. If justice could not be truly blind, he intended to ensure, to the degree that it was possible to ensure, that those who interpreted and administered justice saw it as he did. If this meant pushing the boundaries of the constitutional separation of powers by extending the influence of the president (the executive branch) into the courts (the judicial branch), then so be it. Faced with a choice of blindly embracing the myth of objectivity or accepting with open eyes the realities of human judgment, he chose not to blink.

> **"Company policy," rules,** and laws are written in ink but are applied by minds and hearts moved by the prejudices, desires, threats, and opportunities of a particular time and place. The judgments on which we base actions are never truly objective. Once you accept this reality, endeavor to understand your decision makers as human beings and evaluate the decisions they make in human terms. Never stake money on mythology.

*Lesson 113*
## Measure Deeds, Not People

> "Labor organizations are like other organizations, like organizations of capitalists; sometimes they act very well, and sometimes they act very badly. We should consistently favor them when they act well, and as fearlessly oppose them when they act badly."
>
> ~Editorial in *The Outlook*, 1911

Politicians are perpetually pressured to take sides, meaning to favor one group over or even against another. Theodore Roosevelt refused to be forced into any such static allegiance because he recognized that every organization, as a body both human and social, is of necessity dynamic. It is impossible to judge accurately what a given organization is, but it is imperative that a leader judge what an organization does in a given situation, place, and time.

Roosevelt was willing to take an unequivocal position, provided it was both motivated and limited by actions in a time and in a place. Hence his response to the question of whether or not he sided with labor unions. He began by shattering the apparently self-evident belief that labor unions were essentially the opposite of "organizations of capitalists." Quite the contrary, Roosevelt asserted, they had this in common: "sometimes they act very well and sometimes they act very badly." And that commonality is all the armature he needed, as president, for shaping his policy. Labor unions, like any other organization, including those that naturally oppose them, don't merely *exist*. They *act*. Sometimes they act well. Sometimes they act badly. Roosevelt resolved to build policy on actions, not people.

**All human enterprise is** dynamic; therefore, never make the mistake of chaining yourself to an absolute allegiance based on a fantasy of permanence. Promote, support, or oppose actions, not groups or individuals.

[ 190 ]

## Lesson 114
## Know Your Decision Makers

"A vote is like a rifle: its usefulness depends upon the character of
the user."

~ *An Autobiography*, 1913

Roosevelt well knew that, for the mass of people, the appeal of
democracy resided in the possession of the vote. The vote was a
source of power. The vote was the instrument by which the people
controlled their destiny.

True enough, TR would admit, but, nevertheless, this was not
the whole truth.

The benefits of democracy had to come from something
deeper than the vote, just as the success of a hunt came from
something deeper than a rifle. As the rifle is the instrument of the
hunter, so the vote is the instrument of the citizen. In both cases, the
instruments are indispensable, but, in the end, everything depends
on the "character of the user."

Roosevelt was satisfied that the Constitution and laws of the
United States furnished the tools necessary to build a democratic
republic. As a rifle could not shoot itself, let alone in a manner that
brought down its intended target, so a vote could not vote itself, let
alone cast itself for the candidates who offer the most to preserve,
sustain, enhance, and advance the republic. For this reason,
Roosevelt devoted much attention to the national institutions—
schools, newspapers, journals, libraries, government agencies, and
private businesses—that created the national character. For a
government was only as good as the character of the voters who put
it together and, every two, four, and six years, took it apart and put it
together again.

**Whatever you make, sell,** or serve, your business, like every
other business, is first and last a people business. It will never

be better than the people who build, manage, maintain, develop, and advance it. Give the members of your enterprise the instruments they need to do their jobs, but understand that the usefulness of those instruments depends on the character of those people. They make decisions every day. Know the decisions. Even more important, know the decision makers. Cultivate character.

### Lesson 115
## The Big Stick Revisited

> "If a man continually blusters, if he lacks civility, a big stick will not save him from trouble; and neither will speaking softly avail, if back of the softness there does not lie strength, power."
>
> ~Speech, Minnesota State Fair, September 2, 1901

"Speak softly and carry a big stick" was not only a Roosevelt trademark phrase, but a guide and a favorite for him. This notwithstanding, TR never made the mistake of relying on that stick. Character (or its absence) was in all cases more important than force. Lacking integrity and dignity, a person would soon find the stick of little use, no matter how big it was. This said, integrity and dignity were insufficient to peaceful prosperity without strength and power "back of the softness."

**Authority is impotent without** character, but character cannot assert itself without authority. This is an equation no leader can afford to leave unsolved.

# Lead the Steward's Life

*Lesson 116*
## The Essence of Stewardship

"It is not what we have that will make us a great nation; it is the way in which we use it."
                              ~ Speech, Dickinson, Dakota Territory, July 4, 1886

Theodore Roosevelt took the presidency to a new height of executive power, he took the federal government to a new height of regulatory authority, and he took the United States to a new height of world influence and power. But the majority of historians agree that his most enduring legacy—not only to America but, by the example of the nation, to the world—was his stewardship of natural resources, a movement that in Roosevelt's era was called conservation.

Long before he entered the White House, Roosevelt had come to think of America's forests and wilderness as national treasures to be preserved for the enjoyment of all as well as for their own intrinsic value. When he succeeded to the presidency, he used the bully pulpit of his office to spread the gospel of conservation and to promote a program of conservation legislation, including laws that set aside some 43 million acres of "national forest" to be protected from commercial exploitation either entirely or in part. And when his conservation program collided with congressional representation of farmers and industrialists (who needed water power), prompting Congress to enact legislation in 1908 transferring from the president to Congress the authority to create future national forests in certain western states, TR did not hesitate to use executive orders to circumvent Congress by directly implementing and administering from the White House many of his conservation initiatives.

The root of his commitment to conservation is also the root of his concept of leadership as stewardship. He understood that America possessed natural resources unparalleled in the rest of the world, but he also understood that the nation would be judged not on the basis of its good fortune, but by how it used, how it stewarded, that bounty. Example, whether individual or national, was a compelling moral imperative for Theodore Roosevelt, and the stewardship of natural resources presented a challenge and an opportunity to set an example on a planetary stage.

**No one admires a** corporation or its leaders for their good luck. Both earn the adulation and the loyalty of stakeholders—employees, investors, customers, and even competitors—by the exemplary use they make of whatever fortune gives them.

■

*Lesson 117*
## Call on the Commonplace Virtues

"What is needed is common honesty, common sense, and common courage. We need the minor, the humdrum, the practical virtues—the commonplace virtues that are absolutely essential if we are ever to make this city what it should be. If these virtues are lacking, no amount of cleverness will answer."
~ Speech to the Good Government Club, New York, April 15, 1897

Roosevelt's abiding faith told him that the ordinary conduct of ordinary people was ordinarily decent. Given a chance, honesty, courage, and common sense, he believed, were commonplace. The virtues necessary to good government were not extraordinary, but perfectly ordinary. Crime and corruption, though extensive, were the aberrations, whereas "common decency" was the norm.

Roosevelt held it to be a leader's task to create the conditions that would allow the commonplace virtues to prevail.

**Any organization has its** overachievers and its underachievers. Both groups are outliers, whereas the majority—the ordinary staffers—simply want to achieve. Driven by common honesty, common sense, and common courage, they are inclined to deliver fair work for a fair reward. They want to succeed personally and therefore have an interest in the success of the enterprise. Significantly subpar performance is as exceptional as markedly high levels of performance. Let the success of your enterprise be the product of the common drive of your ordinary employees. Consistently create the conditions that foster the common levels of commitment and productivity. You will almost certainly find this average of achievement to be far higher than you expected.

■

*Lesson 118*
## Deem Denial Fatal

"A Nation should never fight unless forced to; but it should always be ready to fight."
~ Address to the U.S. Naval War College,
Newport, Rhode Island, June 2, 1897

Both as assistant secretary of the navy and as president of the United States, Roosevelt was an unwavering advocate of preparedness for war. This brought some accusations that his policies were provocative at best and even warmongering at worst. Repeatedly, however, Roosevelt asserted his aversion to war and explained in his autobiography that he advocated "preparation for war in order to avert war." Only by demonstrating both a capacity and willingness to fight and win, Roosevelt believed, could the nation hope to deter an enemy assault on its international rights, honor, property, and people. War was undeniably a reality, which could not be avoided by denial. On the contrary, failing to make adequate preparations for war was, Roosevelt believed, a sure way of tempting aggression and even provoking attack.

> **Denying the possibility of** a worst-case scenario will do nothing to avoid it, whereas preparing to manage the worst case may spell the difference between survival and defeat. Denial is based on superstition, whereas preparedness is the product of a rational assessment.

■

## *Lesson 119*
## Draw the Line, Draw It Straight, Draw It Deep

"I thoroughly believe in severe measures when necessary, and am not in the least sensitive about killing any number of men when there is adequate reason, but . . ."

~ Remarks prior to his dismissal of General "Kill and Burn"
Jake Smith, July 14, 1902

After reviewing the transcript of the court martial of U.S. Army general Jake Smith, President Roosevelt summarily fired the popular officer.

Smith had earned the nickname "Kill and Burn" because of the severity of the measures he took against Filipino guerrillas during the so-called insurrection that followed the U.S. annexation of the Philippines after the Spanish-American War. The president had no illusions about the guerrillas, whose torture and mutilation of U.S. soldiers unlucky enough to fall into their hands was notorious, and he was at first inclined to accept the verdict of the court martial, which had been to find Smith guilty of nothing more than "excessive zeal," an offense that merited a mere letter of admonishment. But when Roosevelt personally investigated further, he was appalled to discover that this so-called zeal included killing women and children, a policy Smith called "shooting niggers." This crossed the line from necessary severity to genocidal criminality. Not only was it obscene in itself, Roosevelt decided, such a policy would have a dehumanizing and brutalizing effect on the U.S. Army. He therefore overrode the decision of the court martial and ordered Smith's immediate dismissal not only from command but from the army itself. To his satisfaction, he found that the majority of Smith's fellow officers applauded the action.

> **Draw your straightest,** deepest lines between right and wrong, justice and injustice, the ethical and the unethical. Never cross these, even if you are pushed by custom, policy, standard operating procedure, expediency, or fear. In this you need no company policy, corporate manual, or management ideology to direct you. All that is required is your own sense of decency.

■

*Lesson 120*
## The Most Precious Possession

> "The man who makes a promise which he does not intend to keep, and does not try to keep, should rightly be adjudged to have forfeited . . . what should be every man's most precious possession—his honor."
>
> ~Speech, San Francisco, May 14, 1903

*Honor* is one of those words that, though basic, mark Theodore Roosevelt as a man from another age. It was not necessarily a better age than our own—we still prize honesty, integrity, and character—

but it was less reticent when it came to speaking with a perfectly straight face about personal and public conduct. When Roosevelt spoke of *honor*, turn-of-the-twentieth-century Americans did not have to parse the word. They knew what the president meant by it. Today, however, honor is freighted with subtle shades of connotation Roosevelt and his fellow citizens would have rejected outright.

Why does the word now seem somewhat shallow, pretentious, and naïve? It is not because we are more cynical, but because *honor*, as a concept, has come to be associated, in part, with a certain self-righteous posturing. It is often used as a term expressive less of integrity than of stubborn defiance. People will hold to positions even of dubious value in the name of honor. What some call "honor" prompts the gesture of a shallow dare: *I dare you to cross that line.* In the name of *honor*, many of us cling selfishly to what we claim as "our rights": the right to own as many guns of as many kinds as we desire; the right to be free from all government regulation; the right to a tax cut regardless of the national deficit.

When TR used *honor* the word was far fresher than it is today—crisper and unencumbered. He intended it to express a person's ultimate treasure: a proven, unshakeable reputation for doing what one said one would do.

**For Theodore Roosevelt** and the San Francisco audience who heard him speak in 1903, the word *honor* expressed the moral equivalent of today's 800 credit score. It was a hard-earned passport to absolute trust. Pure gold at the turn of the century, *honor* today is mere currency, and somewhat debased currency at that. It rings hollow in the ear. It represents a value, we know that, but we're no longer quite sure just what value. An unambiguous hot-button concept in Roosevelt's time, *honor* strikes no immediate response today.

Revive it. Purify it. Return it to its original value state.

Define and demonstrate *honor* as your invariable integrity

evident in a perfect one-to-one correspondence between what you promise and what you perform. Repeat this perfect equivalency consistently, and you will achieve in your enterprise the level of vision and efficiency possible only in the presence of genuine honor.

■

*Lesson 121*
## A Square Deal Is a Precise Deal

"A man who is good enough to shed his blood for his country is good enough to be given a square deal afterwards. More than that no man is entitled to, and less than that no man shall have."
~ Speech, Springfield, Illinois, July 4, 1903

President Roosevelt championed veterans' rights, including an adequate pension, not on a vaguely sentimental basis but on the basis of the phrase he used so often: the "square deal."

It was, of course, a phrase hardly original with Roosevelt. Like many other common colloquial expressions, *square deal* is rich in meaning. Consider: No shape or unit of construction is simpler than the square—four equal sides that meet at right angles. Make any side longer or shorter than any other, and you no longer have a square. There is no room for interpretation. There is no ambiguity.

Apply this concept to moral dealings, and you introduce the same level of certainty. A "square deal" was, for Roosevelt, that which a person must be given: "More than that no man is entitled to, and less than that no man shall have." The expression reads equally with the eloquence of an ethical declaration and the self-evident inevitability of a mathematical equation.

**More often than not,** the mark of fairness and justice is the exquisite simplicity of precision. If you cannot express the moral grounds of a decision in clear and unambiguous language, the likelihood is high that the decision is unfair. To hammer out a "square deal," rethink, rewrite, and revise until its language, meaning, and application are precise beyond misunderstanding.

■

*Lesson 122*
## Call to Duty

"If only we can make the man or the woman who, in the home or out of the home, does well his or her hard duty, feel that at least there is a recognition of respect because of that duty being well performed, we shall be by just so much ahead as a nation."
~ Letter to John Hay, August 9, 1903

*Duty* was a favorite word of Theodore Roosevelt, but he also saw the limitation of the duty concept. By definition, a "duty" describes the minimum requirement of a particular job, office, occupation, or even familial role (mother, father, son, or daughter). Although "minimum requirement" is a crucially important dimension of duty, as a definition it also promotes a tendency to take for granted anything called a duty. "Duty" becomes the "least you can do." Recognizing this limitation, Roosevelt expressed his longing for some means of providing a "recognition of respect" for those who perform their duties well. For duty was, in his view, the fulcrum by which the nation was leveraged to greatness.

**Traditional HR management** calls for creating job descriptions that list the "duties" of each employee. These are universally regarded as the minimum requirements of the job. The problem with this view—as Roosevelt clearly saw—was that if we define a duty as a set of minimum expectations, we tend to minimize what is, in fact, the fulcrum on which the enterprise must rise or fall. Better, therefore, to describe a particular job in terms of tasks rather than duties and then define but a single duty: to achieve in these tasks increasingly higher levels of excellence, for which the employee may expect increasingly higher levels of reward in the form of responsibility, authority, and compensation. Discard all "minimum requirements" and replace them with open-ended expectations.

■

*Lesson 123*
## Protect Your Flock

"I wish to call your attention to the fact that there are three parties affected by the situation in the anthracite trade: the operators, the miners, and the general public. I speak for neither the operators nor the miners, but for the general public."

~ To the principals of the coal strike conference
he convened at the White House, October 3, 1902

Turn-of-the-twentieth-century America manufactured, moved, and, above all, heated with coal. Railroads and industry mostly used the softer, less expensive bituminous coal, while the majority of homes and apartments were heated by the harder, hotter, less smoky anthracite. Thus when the United Mine Workers (UMW) struck the anthracite coalfields of eastern Pennsylvania in 1902, the specter of a massive heating-fuel shortage loomed over the threshold of winter. President Roosevelt was faced with a complex crisis. Historically, presidents did not intervene in labor matters. Should he? *Could* he—legally? And if he did intervene, with whom should or could he side? Labor (the miners) or the operators (the mine owners)? Finally, if labor and operators failed to resolve their differences, what federal power could the president bring to bear in order to avert a coal famine in the dead of winter?

The strike commenced on May 12, 1902. Soon, some 80 percent of Pennsylvania anthracite miners had walked off the job—about 100,000 men. When violence erupted between strikers and strikebreakers, the owners called in police as well as hired Pinkerton security guards, and the governor called out the Pennsylvania National Guard. Unwilling to act rashly, President Roosevelt ordered on June 8 his commissioner of labor, Carroll D. Wright, to investigate the strike and report to him on it. The commissioner recommended yielding to UMW demands for a nine-hour day, at least on a trial basis, and some form of collective bargaining. Modest though these recommendations were, Roosevelt decided to withhold the report for the time being, so as not to appear to be siding with the union. He did not want to sacrifice the appearance of his unbiased neutrality, which would be useful if he were to arbitrate the dispute. But as the days went by, Roosevelt, fearing a winter coal famine, finally proposed to intervene directly. When his attorney general advised him that he had no constitutional authority to do so, Roosevelt took what he considered the next best step by convening, under his auspices as president, a conference of representatives of government, labor, and management on October 3, 1902.

The president made clear to the conference that he spoke for the interests of the general public, not the union and not the owners; however, he did try to persuade the UMW to end the strike by promising to create a permanent commission and pledging to support whatever measures the commission proposed. UMW president John Mitchell refused. With this avenue closed, Roosevelt prevailed upon financier J. P. Morgan—against whom he had earlier initiated antitrust action—to propose a compromise. Morgan suggested that the commission be used to arbitrate an end to the strike by providing a channel for the two sides to negotiate without the owners having to surrender to bargaining directly with the union. The compromise worked, and the 163-day-old strike ended on October 23, 1902. As the president had earlier promised, the Anthracite Coal Commission studied the industry, held extensive hearings, and ultimately arrived at a compromise that essentially split the difference between what the miners demanded and the owners were willing to give.

For the first time in American history, the U.S. president became directly involved in labor, yet he did so without appearing to yield to one side or the other. Instead, as he had declared, he represented the interests and welfare of the "general public."

> **Define your constituency** and deal with everyone else in a manner that satisfies them to the greatest possible degree while serving without compromise those for whom it is your duty to speak. The reality as well as the appearance of fairness must begin as well as end with absolute clarity.

■

*Lesson 124*
## Avoid Risk
## (without the Prospect of Worthwhile Reward)

> "I do not in the least object to your getting smashed if it is for an
> object that is worthwhile, such as playing on the Groton [football]
> team or playing on your class team when you get to Harvard. But
> I think it a little silly to run any imminent risk of a serious smash
> simply to play on the second squad instead of the third."
>
> ~Letter to his son Theodore Jr., October 11, 1903

Advocate of "the strenuous life," Roosevelt nevertheless drew the line at taking a risk for risk's sake. The prospect of significant benefit, however, might well make a risk worthwhile, as the president explained to his son. Risk without a valuable object was not courageous, but foolhardy. "If an individual starts to play football," Roosevelt told an audience of Occidental College students in Los Angeles on March 22, 1911, "and expects not to get bumped, he will be sadly disappointed." It was, he believed, essential to have a full understanding of the risks as well as the potential rewards before embarking on anything dangerous, painful, or otherwise costly. Risking life and limb to gain prominence on a varsity team was of value because, in years to come, people of standing would recognize that value and, quite possibly, reward it. It was a way to earn credibility in the society of powerful men.

**Theodore Roosevelt habitually pushed** himself physically and mentally. He deliberately shunned the comfortable life for "the strenuous life." Yet, whatever he undertook, he was first and last a conservationist, who was loath to spend himself foolishly.

Rule of thumb: Presented with a risk, avoid it. Presented with an opportunity entailing risk, weigh them both with the intention of engaging the risk unless it clearly outweighs the benefit. If it does, walk on to the next opportunity.

■

*Lesson 125*
## Power Strategy: Accept Responsibility

"Much has been given to us, and much will rightfully be expected from us. We have duties to others and duties to ourselves; and we can shirk neither. We have become a great Nation, forced by the fact of its greatness into relations with the other nations of the earth; and we must behave as beseems a people with such responsibilities."

~Inaugural address, March 4, 1905

Reluctantly, Theodore Roosevelt's predecessor in the White House, William McKinley, led the United States into position as a world power when he yielded to congressional and popular calls for intervention in Cuba and the Philippines against the Spanish empire. As president, Roosevelt built on this overture to more fully establish the United States as an international player. He began his elected term in 1905 by acknowledging the nation's new role in the world, a role that brought great benefits ("much has been given us") and great responsibilities ("duties to others").

Depending on the political fashion of the day, President Roosevelt has been both hailed and condemned in the century-plus since 1905 for his foreign policy. Some have praised it as altruistically visionary, others as crassly imperialistic. We need not continue the debate here, but it is important to examine the significance of the dual nature of world power as he presented it: a set of benefits balanced by a set of responsibilities. In the inaugural address, the responsibilities—"duties"—come across as the inevitable moral cost of the benefits. The United States *owes* these costs and owes them without question.

Doubtless, President Roosevelt sincerely believed in the equation he presented, yet it is hard not to see in it something of an ulterior motive. The duties that the president defines as costs are also motives for expanding, broadening, and deepening American power in the world. Giving back requires taking more. In the name of discharging the nation's responsibility, it becomes the nation's responsibility to acquire yet *more* influence and power in the world. In TR's vision of America's international destiny, duty and responsibility were requirements that never constrained but, on the contrary, expanded. Instead of limiting diplomatic action, they

[207]

licensed and liberated it. He transformed duty from obligation to enabler.

> **Find ways to make** doing the *right* thing the *profitable* thing, the thing that builds the enterprise and projects it deeper and deeper into the marketplace. Join opportunity to duty and thereby prosper.

■

### Lesson 126
## Actions Speak Louder

> "The man who utters moral sentiments to which he does not try to live up, and the other man who listens and applauds the utterance of those sentiments and yet himself does not try to live up to them—both those men not only gain no good from what they have said and listened to, but have done themselves positive harm, because they have weakened just a little the spring of conscience within them."
>
> ~Speech to Harvard Union, Harvard University, February 23, 1907

Theodore Roosevelt was a prolific writer and a voluble talker, but he was a *great* doer. Impressive though his command of English was, his command of the language of action was greater by far. In deeds he spoke more loudly and more clearly than in words, and, what is more, he demanded the same of everyone who occupied or bid to occupy a position of responsibility.

> **A leader must be** a communicator. The most compelling language she can speak consists of the actions she takes, the decisions she executes, the opportunities she realizes, the problems she solves, and the policies she enforces. Old-time

U.S. Navy officers sought to transform their verbal commands into absolute action by following each order with the phrase Make it so. Make it so.

■

*Lesson 127*
## Never Allow the Best to Become the Enemy of the Good

"We know that there are in life injustices which we are powerless to remedy. But we also know that there is much injustice which can be remedied."

~Speech at Madison Square Garden, New York, October 30, 1912

The architect of the modern German empire, Otto von Bismarck, famously defined politics as "the art of the possible." Despite the intensity of his own idealistic ambition and his zeal as a political reformer, Roosevelt eagerly assented to this view. "When we undertake the impossible," he told an audience in Chicago on September 3, 1900, "we often fail to do anything at all." He understood all too well, as he had observed years earlier in a speech at Buffalo, New York, on January 26, 1893, that the "man who goes into politics should not expect to reform everything right off, with a jump."

**Idealism, TR believed, was** a quality indispensable in a leader. At the same time, idealism was useless unless it could be put into real and practical action. Often, this meant seizing the proverbial half a loaf rather than insisting on the whole and ending up with none. To turn your back on the good because it is not the best is a waste of opportunity and a dereliction of duty. To achieve nothing because you cannot achieve everything is the very definition of failure.

■

*Lesson 128*
## Lead Emphatically

"While President, I have been President, emphatically."

~Letter to Sir George Otto Trevelyan, June 19, 1908

After leaving office, President Roosevelt cheerfully admitted to having used "every ounce of power there was in the office" of president. As for "the criticism of those who spoke of 'usurpation of power,'" he had "not cared a rap." He believed that his use of the office was not only "right in itself, but that in showing the strength of, or in giving strength to, the executive, [he] was establishing a precedent of value." His purpose was not to become powerful, but to leave the office of president more powerful than he had found it. "I believe," he declared, "in a strong executive; I believe in power ... but I believe that the strong executive should be a perpetual executive." The strength should be a property of the office, not just an attribute of the particular individual who occupies the office at any given time.

Not since the very first president, George Washington, and the seventh, Andrew Jackson, had a president regarded himself so thoroughly a steward of the office he held. Theodore Roosevelt set out to redefine the office—and in particular to expand its power—beyond his own tenure. His intention was to bequeath to his successors a more powerful presidency. The Constitution, after all, says remarkably little about the extent and the limits of executive office, and therefore, like Washington and Jackson before him, Roosevelt believed that it was both his opportunity and his responsibility to add to the definition of the executive by means of the precedent of action. This required him to be "President emphatically" and to use the office to its very utmost, leaving its boundaries stretched larger than when he had succeeded President McKinley.

**As CEO, supervisor, or** manager, you don't merely fill the position you hold, you define it by your decisions, policies, and actions. You have a responsibility to be a good steward of your entire organization, including your very own office. Theodore Roosevelt's concept of stewardship was to grow the power of the executive.

Do you want to leave your office larger or smaller? Should it be predominantly executive or administrative? There is no guaranteed right answer. Many of Roosevelt's predecessors as well as successors used the office differently from the way he used it. The great object, however, is to understand that what you do creates a definition that will outlast your tenure. The best you can do for the future of your organization is to approach this long act of definition consciously, deliberately, and, above all, emphatically.

■

*Lesson 129*
## The Danger of Efficiency

"If a man's efficiency is not guided and regulated by a moral sense, then the more efficient he is . . . the more dangerous to the body politic."

~Speech, Sorbonne, Paris, April 23, 1910

Anyone who encountered Theodore Roosevelt was impressed, first, foremost, and—sometimes—also last, by the sheer energy of the man.

William Sturgis Bigelow, physician and celebrated American expert on Japanese culture, observed that he had never seen anyone like TR, "a man with such a head of steam on." Another Roosevelt friend observed that the president "never stops running, even while he stokes and fires." In an industrial age on the cusp of Henry Ford's hyper-efficient assembly line, an age in love with efficiency and always determined to squeeze out even more of it, TR seemed the ideal man of the hour. Always doing, he never had a minute to waste.

Without doubt, Roosevelt valued efficiency highly, as he valued force itself. Nevertheless, he understood that efficiency, like force, required the guidance and control of a morally intelligent hand. Without such governance, raw efficiency was a power of potentially limitless destruction. Those who were just coming of age in the Teddy Roosevelt era would live to see precisely what the former president meant when, in 1910, he warned of the danger to the body politic posed by efficiency in the absence of "a moral sense." Two qualities would mark the regimes of Adolf Hitler and Joseph Stalin beginning some twenty years later: a limitless want of morality and a limitless capacity for efficiency.

**Business has always been** infatuated with the bottom-line manager. Whenever you are tempted to become one, take careful note of the key quantity no balance sheet ever tallies. It may be called ethics, justice, good corporate citizenship, doing the right thing. Or it may be called "a moral sense."

■

## Lesson 130
## Achieve Ethical Efficiency

"I have mighty little use for ethics that are applied with such inefficiency that no good results come."

~Speech, Harvard University, December 14, 1910

Theodore Roosevelt would never advise anyone to "aspire to act ethically." He would advise everyone simply "to act ethically." For him, no enterprise could satisfy itself with ethical aspirations any more than a business could satisfy itself with aspirations to profit. Ethics had to be achieved in fact and with efficiency—the same efficiency a business devoted to innovation, production, promotion, and sales for the purpose of creating prosperity.

**The closing decade of** the twentieth century and the opening decade of the twenty-first have taught business that ethics cannot be a corporate aspiration. It must be a corporate reality. Stewardship, integrity, and trust are no longer optional (if they ever really were) but must be integral to any business plan. Supervisors, managers, and CEOs need to value, present, and enforce ethics as absolutely as they value, present, and enforce the bottom line.

**Lesson 131**
## Establish a Hierarchy of Rights

> "The man who wrongly holds that every human right is secondary to his profit must now give way to the advocate of human welfare, who rightly maintains that every man holds his property subject to the general right of the community to regulate its use to whatever degree the public welfare may require it."
>
> ~ *The New Nationalism*, 1910

Central to the problem of leading a free nation, Theodore Roosevelt decided, was reconciling individual rights with the rights of the nation as a community. He defined as a responsibility of the federal government the defense of the national community's "right to regulate" the use of individual property "to whatever degree the public welfare may require it." Absent the recognition of this communal right, "every human right" becomes secondary to individual profit. Allow this to happen, and the nation ceases to be a community. Ceasing to be a free nation, it becomes instead a fiefdom of large property holders.

**The leader of any** organization must moderate between the rights of individual members of the organization and the rights of the organization as a whole. Typically, this requires "regulating"—directing, guiding, ordering—individual actions to ensure that they contribute to the collective objectives of the organization. In business, much of the art of leadership is in carrying out this regulation without discouraging or altogether extinguishing individual initiative and creativity. Generally, the most effective leadership tools are those that focus everyone's attention on clearly defined goals for the enterprise and stimulate individual contributions toward these common goals.

*Lesson 132*
## Character Is Destiny

> "The United States of America has not the option as to whether
> it will or will not play a great part in the world. It must play a
> great part."
>
> ~ *The Outlook*, April 1, 1911

Some five hundred years before the birth of Christ, the Greek philosopher Heraclitus of Ephesus proposed that "character is destiny." What you are is what you must, through your own actions, inevitably become. We may debate this provocative theorem, but Theodore Roosevelt chose instead to use something very like it when he described an American destiny determined by the American character. Having matured into a great world power, he said, the United States no longer possessed the option to evade its destiny. The nation had no choice but to "play a great part" in the world.

> **Roosevelt deftly branded** the United States a world power, thereby laying out a destiny of deep engagement in the affairs of nations. As he demonstrated, defining character, whether of an individual or an organization, is a compelling form of branding, which, in turn, is a powerful means of outlining the destiny of a person or an enterprise.

■

*Lesson 133*
## Regulate Power with Power

> "It is essential that there should be organizations of labor. . . .
> Capital organizes and therefore labor must organize."
>
> ~ Speech, Milwaukee, October 14, 1912

The speech third-party presidential candidate Theodore Roosevelt delivered with a would-be assassin's bullet lodged in his chest was largely about the management of power. More specifically, it was about the necessity in a democracy of balancing power against power. He declared his belief that labor not only had a right to organize into unions, but a responsibility to do so for the simple reason that capital was organized. The balance of one force against another force was the way of nature and, as Roosevelt saw it, this also had to be the way of institutions in a democratic society. Such a scheme of dynamically balanced opposition would not increase strife, but, on the contrary, tend to create an equilibrium in which neither side could tyrannize over the other.

> **As a leadership tool,** power is neither to be feared nor avoided. Every stakeholder in your organization—employees, bosses, investors, clients, customers—wields power. Your leadership task is to create a productive equilibrium among the various forces in your enterprise. Apply power to manage power.

■

### Lesson 134
## Make Every Deal a Square Deal

"We demand that big business give the people a square deal; in return we must insist that when anyone engaged in big business honestly endeavors to do right he shall himself be given a square deal."

~Editorial in *The Outlook*, November 18, 1911

Before the New Deal of his fifth cousin Franklin Delano Roosevelt, who would serve as U.S. president from 1933 until his death in April 1945, there was Theodore Roosevelt's own "Square Deal," the catch phrase by which he labeled his domestic agenda promoting conservation of natural resources, regulation of corporate big business, and federal protection of consumers. Under the aegis of the Square Deal, TR earned the nickname of "Trust Buster," because of his aggressive enforcement of legislation aimed at dismantling an emerging American plutocracy of big "trusts"–as massively monopolistic corporations were called.

As most Americans saw it at the time, and as many historians still see it, opposition to big business run amok was the essence of the Square Deal. This, however, was only two sides of the square. Even as TR sought to protect the middle class from the plutocratic tyranny of big business unchecked by competition and federal regulation, so he sought to protect business itself from what he deemed the radical demands of certain aspects of organized labor. Roosevelt's approach to big business embodied his understanding of the very root of all business: the exchange of value for value. It was no more radical or complex than the Golden Rule translated into the terms of commerce. The government and the people had a right to *demand* a square deal from business provided that business received in return a square deal from government and the people.

> **The "square deal" is** not the kindest, nicest, or best model for business, but it is the only reliably sustainable one. A business enterprise built on anything less than the concept of the square deal—the commitment and intention to deliver value for value received—is not, in fact, a business at all, but more in the nature of a criminal enterprise. To take value without delivering value in return is theft.

**Lesson 135**
## Be Truly Conservative

"The only true conservative is the man who resolutely sets his face toward the future."

~Roosevelt quoted by John Morton Blum in
*The Republican Roosevelt,* 1954

As a historical figure, Theodore Roosevelt has had the dubious distinction of rejection by superficial liberals as well as superficial conservatives. The liberals have derided him as autocratic and imperialistic, the conservatives as an advocate of federal regulation run wild. The truth was that TR identified himself neither as liberal nor conservative, but as *progressive.*

In recent years, the word *progressive* has been adopted by the political left to describe itself. There can be no denying that much of the Roosevelt agenda would today be hailed—or condemned—as "progressive" in that modern liberal sense. He was the original "green" president, of course, and he was a political reformer, who believed that the business of government was, in the language of the Preamble to the Constitution, "to promote the general welfare." For him, this meant endowing the federal government with powerful regulatory authority, especially where big business was concerned.

Yet Roosevelt would never have branded his "progressivism" as liberal. If anything, he saw himself as conservative in what he held to be the true sense of the word and the concept. As he saw it, a conservative leader did not avoid change or seek to undo change by looking to the past, but, on the contrary, resolutely "set his face toward the future," with an eye toward conserving—defending, preserving, protecting, and promoting—what is best and most important to the nation. A true conservative understood that the conditions of life are restless and dynamic, ceaselessly offering both opportunity and challenge. As a true conservative, TR knew he could not resist this dynamism anymore than he could resist gravity or any other natural force. Instead of trying in vain to resist, he looked ahead for ways to cope with and take advantage of the dynamism and opportunities for change, his object always being to carry the country forward.

> **Rethink what it means** to be "conservative." Roosevelt believed the "true conservative" was committed to the future with the object of ensuring the ongoing prosperity of her enterprise—not by looking backward in a futile attempt to resist change or hold onto the past, but by looking forward to anticipate threats and challenges as well as recognize new vistas: the opportunities to grow and prosper beyond mere survival.

■

## Lesson 136
## Evaluate the Bottom Line at the Very Bottom

"When I left the presidency, I finished seven and a half years of administration, during which not one shot had been fired against a foreign foe. We were at absolute peace, and there was no nation in the world . . . whom we had wronged, or from whom we had anything to fear."

~ *An Autobiography*, 1913

President Roosevelt was determined to claim for America a preeminent place on the planet. For this, he was often criticized as an imperialist, a jingoist, and even a warmonger. He did not engage in a quibbling contest over such words. He made no excuses for his actions and policies. He made no attempt to spin results to create a favorable impression. Instead, like a skilled accountant, he found the very bottom of the bottom line of his presidency, and he let it speak for itself, without shading, color, or comment.

**Monitor progress and** assess achievement in the most basic and essential terms possible. Determine what really counts, then measure your record against this and only this.

■

# A TR Timeline

**1858**
October 27: Born in New York City.

**1876–80**
Attends Harvard College, graduating June 30, 1880, magna cum
laude.

**1877**
First published book appears, *The Summer Birds of the
Adirondacks*.

**1878**
February 9: Theodore Roosevelt Sr. (father) dies.

**1880–82**
Attends Columbia Law School, leaving without taking a degree;
never practices law.

**1880**

Becomes active in Republican politics.

October 27: Marries Alice Hathaway Lee.

**1881**

November 8: Becomes the youngest member ever elected
to New York State Assembly, winning 3,490 votes to his
opponent's 1,989.

**1882**

Publishes *The Naval War of 1812*, which is adopted as a required
textbook by the U.S. Naval Academy.

August 1: Joins the National Guard (commissioned a second
lieutenant in B Company of New York's 8th Regiment).

**1883**

November 6: Reelected to the New York State Assembly by a
landslide—a margin wider than that of any other New York state
legislator—and is elected minority leader. During this term, he
tours New York City slums with labor leader Samuel Gompers;
authors public welfare legislation.

**1883–84**

Purchases land and creates the Maltese Cross and Elkhorn cattle
ranches in Dakota Territory (modern North Dakota).

**1884**

February 12: Alice Lee Roosevelt born.

February 14: Martha Bulloch Roosevelt (Roosevelt's mother)
dies of typhoid fever a few hours before Roosevelt's wife,
Alice Hathaway Lee Roosevelt, succumbs to Bright's disease.

His daughter's birth and the deaths of his mother and his wife all take place in his 57th Street Manhattan home.

March: Construction of the house Roosevelt will name Sagamore Hill begins in Oyster Bay, Long Island. The home is completed the following year.

June: Serves as delegate to the Republican National Convention.

**1885**
Publishes *Hunting Trips of a Ranchman*, an account of his rugged life in the Dakota Badlands. Leaves the New York State Assembly after his third term.

**1886**
November 2: Defeated for New York City mayor by Democrat Abram S. Hewitt.
December 2: Marries Edith Kermit Carow.

**1887**
Publishes *Life of Thomas Hart Benton*.
September 13: Theodore Jr. born at Sagamore Hill.

**1888**
Publishes *Life of Gouverneur Morris, Ranch Life and the Hunting Trail,* and *Essays in Practical Politics*.

**1889**
Publishes *The Winning of the West,* volumes 1 and 2 (volume 3 appears in 1894, and volume 4, 1896).
May 7: Appointed U.S. civil service commissioner, Washington, D.C. (serves until May 5, 1895).

October 10: Kermit Roosevelt born at Sagamore Hill.

## 1891

Publishes *History of New York*.

August 13: Ethel Carow Roosevelt born at Sagamore Hill.

## 1893

Publishes *The Wilderness Hunter*.

## 1894

April 10: Archibald Bulloch Roosevelt born in Washington, D.C.

August 14: Elliott Roosevelt (brother; father of future first lady Eleanor Roosevelt) dies of injuries following a suicide attempt.

## 1895

Publishes *Hero Tales from American History* (coauthor, Senator Henry Cabot Lodge).

May 5: Resigns as U.S. civil service commissioner.

May 6: Appointed president of the Board of Police Commissioners, New York City; serves through April 19, 1897.

## 1897

Publishes *American Ideals*.

April 19: Resigns from New York City Police Board to accept appointment by President William McKinley as assistant secretary of the navy.

November 19: Quentin Roosevelt, born in Washington, D.C.

## 1898

May 6: Resigns as assistant secretary of the navy to accept appointment as lieutenant colonel, 1st U.S. Volunteer Cavalry days after commencement of the Spanish-American War.

May 15–September 16: Serves as lieutenant colonel and then colonel of the Rough Riders.

June 24: First firefight, battle of Las Guasimas, Cuba.

July 1: Leads the Rough Riders to a bloody victory at the decisive battle of San Juan Hill (a.k.a battles of San Juan Heights and Kettle Hill); although nominated for a Medal of Honor, he does not receive it until it is awarded posthumously in 2001.

August 14: Returns to the United States and is quarantined with his regiment for six weeks at Camp Wikoff (Montauk, Long Island, New York).

September 27: The war hero is nominated by the Republican Party for New York governor.

November 8: Elected governor, winning 661,715 votes versus 643,921 for Democrat Augustus Van Wyck.

## 1899

Publishes *The Rough Riders*.

January 2: Inaugurated as New York governor; serves until December 31, 1900.

## 1900

November 6: Elected vice president of the United States on the Republican ticket with William McKinley. The victory owes much to his campaigning, which is much more vigorous than McKinley's. The ticket receives 7,219,530 votes versus 6,358,071 for the Democrat's William Jennings Bryan and Adlai E. Stevenson.

## 1901

March 4–September 14: Serves as vice president of the United States.

September 6: President William McKinley is shot at Buffalo, New York; assured that the president will recover, Vice President Roosevelt continues a hiking vacation at remote Mount Tahawus in New York's Adirondacks.

September 14: When President McKinley dies of his wounds, Roosevelt rushes to Buffalo and is sworn in as the nation's twenty-sixth president. At age forty-two, he is the youngest to serve.

## 1902

February 19: Embarks on "trust-busting" campaign, ordering Attorney General Philander Knox to bring suit against the monopolistic Northern Securities Company under the Sherman Antitrust Act. The Roosevelt administration will bring an additional forty-four antitrust suits against other monopolies.

May 22: Establishes Crater Lake National Park in Oregon, the first of five national parks he will create: Wind Cave National Park, South Dakota, 1903; Sullys Hill National Park (today, Sullys Hill National Game Preserve), North Dakota, 1904; Platt National Park, Oklahoma, 1906; and Mesa Verde National Park, Colorado, 1906.

June 17: Signs the Newlands Reclamation Act, monumental conservation legislation that will lead to twenty-one more major federal irrigation projects.

June 28: Signs the Isthmian Canal Act, authorizing construction of the Panama Canal.

October 15: Roosevelt sets the precedent for the chief executive's intervention in disputes between labor and capital by mediating settlement of the great anthracite coal strike.

December 31: Roosevelt exercises "Big Stick" diplomacy in his resolution of the Venezuelan Crisis.

## 1903

February 14: Creates the Department of Commerce and Labor as part of the cabinet.

February 19: Signs the Elkins Act, imposing fines on livestock and petroleum interests that extorted rebates from railroads; a cornerstone of Roosevelt's "Square Deal" domestic doctrine.

March 14: Proclaims Pelican Island, Florida, as a federal bird reservation—first of fifty-one he will set aside during his administration.

November 13: Roosevelt rushes to recognize the independence of Panama from Colombia, paving the way to a treaty enabling construction of the Panama Canal.

November 18: A treaty is concluded with Panama for building the Panama Canal.

December 17: Signs a Cuban reciprocity treaty, making Cuba a quasi-client of the United States.

## 1904

November 8: Roosevelt is elected in his own right, defeating Democrat Alton B. Parker, 7,628,834 votes to 5,084,401.

December 6: Promulgates the "Roosevelt Corollary" to the Monroe Doctrine, asserting the U.S. right to intervene in the economic affairs of Latin American states unable or unwilling to pay their international debts.

## 1905

Publishes *Outdoor Pastimes of an American Hunter.*

February 1: Establishes the National Forest Service.

March 4: Inaugurated.

March 17: Gives away niece Eleanor Roosevelt at the ceremony of her wedding to Franklin Delano Roosevelt.

June 2: Establishes Wichita Forest in Oklahoma as the first federal game preserve. (In 1908 he will create Grand Canyon federal game preserve followed in 1909 by Fire Island, Alaska, and the National Bison Range, Montana.)

September 5: Mediates peace between Russia and Japan (Treaty of Portsmouth), ending the Russo-Japanese War.

## 1906

January: At the Algeciras Conference, resolves differences between France and Germany over Morocco; not only is Moroccan independence preserved, but so is the European balance of power.

February 17: The nation is thrilled by the White House wedding of Roosevelt's wildly popular daughter, Alice, to Ohio congressman Nicholas Longworth.

June 8: Signs the Antiquities (or National Monuments) Act, creating the first of eighteen designated "National Monuments," including Devils Tower (1906), Muir Woods (1908), Grand Canyon (1908), and Mount Olympus (1909).

June 11: Signs the Forest Homestead Act, providing that forest land chiefly valuable for agriculture may be occupied and patented as a homestead.

June 29: Signs the Hepburn Act, which gives the Interstate Commerce Commission authority to regulate railroad rates.

June 30: Signs the Pure Food and Drug Act and a federal meat inspection law, milestones in federal consumer health and welfare protection.

November 8–26: Accompanied by his wife, inspects progress on the Panama Canal; it is the first time a U.S. president ventures outside of the country while in office.

December 10: Awarded the Nobel Peace Prize for his role in ending the Russo-Japanese War.

December 16: Sends the navy's "Great White Fleet" on a spectacular circumnavigation to demonstrate U.S. sea power.

## 1908

May 13–15: Hosts a White House conference of governors to discuss issues of conservation.

June 8: Appoints a National Conservation Commission to draw up an inventory of America's natural resources.

## 1909

February 18: Convenes the North American Conservation Conference at the White House.

February 22: The "Great White Fleet" triumphantly returns, completing its circumnavigation.

March 4: Roosevelt's handpicked successor, William Howard Taft, is inaugurated.

## 1909–10

March 1909–June 1910: Leads a major African hunting expedition to collect specimens for Smithsonian Institution, and then tours Europe to great popular acclaim.

## 1910

May 20: Appointed special ambassador to Great Britain for the funeral of King Edward VII.

June 18: Returns to the United States; soon afterward publishes *African Game Trails*.

August 31: Delivers iconic "New Nationalism" address, Osawatomie, Kansas.

## 1911

Becomes an editor for *The Outlook* magazine.

## 1912

Publishes *Realizable Ideals*.

February 21: Deeply dissatisfied with the conservative Taft administration, throws his "hat in the ring" for the Republican nomination.

June 18–22: Although Roosevelt wins all but one primary and caucus, the Republican National Convention re-nominates incumbent Taft.

August 5–7: The new National Progressive Party (better known as the "Bull Moose Party") nominates Roosevelt.

October 14: As he prepares to make a campaign speech in Milwaukee, would-be assassin John Schrank shoots him point-blank in the chest. Passing through the candidate's speech manuscript and deflected by an eyeglasses case, the bullet lodges superficially in his chest, and Roosevelt insists on giving a ninety-minute speech before he consents to be taken to the hospital.

November 5: Comes in second behind Democrat Woodrow Wilson but ahead of Republican Taft, taking 27.4 percent of the popular vote.


## 1913

Publishes *Theodore Roosevelt: An Autobiography* and *History as Literature and Other Essays*.

October 4: Embarks on a South American lecture tour and jungle expedition.


## 1914

February 27–April 27: Sponsored by the American Museum of Natural History and the government of Brazil, the Roosevelt-Rondon Expedition explores Brazil's "River of Doubt," which is renamed "Rio Roosevelt" (and is sometimes called "Rio Teodoro"). On his return to the United States, publishes *Through the Brazilian Wilderness* and coauthors *Life-Histories of African Game Animals*.

## 1915

January 1: Publishes *America and the World War*, an argument against U.S. neutrality.

## 1916

Publishes *A Booklover's Holidays in the Open* and *Fear God and Take Your Own Part*.

June 10: Progressive (Bull Moose) Party nominates Theodore Roosevelt, who declines the nomination and instead backs Republican nominee Charles Evans Hughes.

## 1917

May 19: President Woodrow Wilson turns down Roosevelt's request that he be allowed to raise and lead a volunteer unit for service in the Great War.

## 1918

Publishes *The Great Adventure*.

July: Declines Republican nomination for governor of New York.

July 14: Youngest son Quentin, an aviator, is killed over the trenches of France.

## 1919

January 6: Dies in his sleep, age sixty. The cause is a coronary embolism.

# Bibliography

Alfonso, Oscar M. *Theodore Roosevelt and the Philippines, 1897–1909.* New York: Oriole, 1974.

Berman, Jay Stuart. *Police Administration and Progressive Reform: Theodore Roosevelt as Police Commissioner of New York.* Westport, Conn.: Greenwood, 1987.

Bishop, Joseph Bucklin. *Theodore Roosevelt and His Time.* 2 vols. New York: C. Scribner's Sons, 1920.

Blum, John Morton. *The Republican Roosevelt.* Cambridge, Mass.: Harvard University Press, 1954.

Brands, H. W. T. R.: *The Last Romantic.* New York: Basic Books, 1997.

Chambers, John Whiteclay. *The Tyranny of Change: America in the Progressive Era, 1890–1920.* 2nd ed. New Brunswick, N.J.: Rutgers University Press, 2000.

Collin, Richard H. *Theodore Roosevelt's Caribbean: The Panama Canal, the Monroe Doctrine, and the Latin American Context.* Baton Rouge: Louisiana State University Press, 1990.

Cornell, Robert J. *The Anthracite Coal Strike of 1902.* 1957; reprint ed., New York: Russell & Russell, 1971.

Dalton, Kathleen. *Theodore Roosevelt: A Strenuous Life.* New York: Alfred A. Knopf, 2002.

Diaz Espino, Ovidio. *How Wall Street Created a Nation: J.P. Morgan, Teddy Roosevelt, and the Panama Canal.* New York: Four Walls Eight Windows, 2001.

DiNunzio, Mario R., ed. *Theodore Roosevelt: An American Mind.* New York: Penguin, 1994.

Dyer, Thomas G. *Theodore Roosevelt and the Idea of Race.* Baton Rouge: Louisiana State University Press, 1980.

Ferleger, Herbert Ronald, and Albert Bushnell Hart. *Theodore Roosevelt Cyclopedia.* Westport, Conn.: Meckler Corporation and Theodore Roosevelt Association, 1988.

Gable, John A. *The Bull Moose Years: Theodore Roosevelt and the Progressive Party.* Port Washington, N.Y.: Kennikat Press, 1978.

Gould, Lewis L. *Reform and Regulation: American Politics from Roosevelt to Wilson.* 3rd ed. Prospect Heights, Ill.: Waveland Press, 1996.

———. *The Presidency of Theodore Roosevelt.* Lawrence: University Press of Kansas, 1991.

Hannigan, Robert E. *The New World Power: American Foreign Policy, 1898–1917.* Philadelphia: University of Pennsylvania Press, 2002.

Hay, Samuel P. *Conservation and the Gospel of Efficiency: The Progressive Conservation Movement, 1890–1920.* Cambridge, Mass.: Harvard University Press, 1959.

Hunt, John Gabriel, ed. *The Essential Theodore Roosevelt.* New York: Gramercy Books, 1994.

Jeffers, H. Paul. *The Bully Pulpit: A Teddy Roosevelt Book of Quotations.* Dallas, Tex.: Taylor Publishing Company, 1998.

McCullough, David G. *Mornings on Horseback.* New York: Simon and Schuster, 1981.

———. *The Path between the Seas: The Creation of the Panama Canal, 1870–1914.* New York: Simon and Schuster, 1977.

Meyer, Balthasar Henry. *A History of the Northern Securities Case.* New York: Da Capo Press, 1972.

Morris, Edmund. *Colonel Roosevelt.* New York: Random House, 2011.

———. *The Rise of Theodore Roosevelt.* 1979; reprint ed., New York: Random House, 2010.

———. *Theodore Rex.* New York: Random House, 2001.

Mowry, George E. *The Era of Theodore Roosevelt, 1900–1912.* New York: Harper, 1958.

Neu, Charles E. *An Uncertain Friendship: Theodore Roosevelt and Japan, 1906–1909.* Cambridge, Mass.: Harvard University Press, 1967.

O'Gara, Gordon Carpenter. *Theodore Roosevelt and the Rise of the Modern Navy.* New York: Greenwood Press, 1969.

Pringle, Henry F. *Theodore Roosevelt: A Biography.* New York: Harcourt Brace, 1931.

Reckner, James R. *Teddy Roosevelt's Great White Fleet.* Annapolis, Md.: Naval Institute Press, 1988.

Robinson, Corinne Roosevelt. *My Brother, Theodore Roosevelt.* New York: Charles Scribner's Sons, 1921.

Rodgers, Daniel T. *Atlantic Crossings: Social Politics in a Progressive Age.* Cambridge, Mass.: Harvard University Press, 1998.

Roosevelt, Theodore. *An Autobiography.* 1913; reprint ed., New York: Da Capo, 1985.

———. *The Selected Letters of Theodore Roosevelt.* Edited by H. W. Brands. New York: Cooper Square Press, 2001.

———. *The Works of Theodore Roosevelt.* Memorial ed., 24 vols. Edited by Hermann Hagedorn. New York: Scribner's, 1926.

Trani, Eugene P. *The Treaty of Portsmouth: An Adventure in American Diplomacy.* Lexington: University of Kentucky Press, 1969.

Wimmel, Kenneth. *Theodore Roosevelt and the Great White Fleet: American Sea Power Comes of Age.* Washington, D.C.: Brassey's, 1998.

Young, James Harvey. *Pure Food: Securing the Federal Food and Drugs Act of 1906.* Princeton, N.J.: Princeton University Press, 1989.

# Lesson Index

## 1 LEAD THE STRENUOUS LIFE

## Lesson 11
Dare **39**

*"Far better it is to dare mighty things, to win glorious triumphs, even though checkered by failure, than to take rank with those poor spirits who neither enjoy much nor suffer much, because they live in the gray twilight that knows not victory nor defeat."*

## Lesson 12
Lead the Strenuous Life–and More **40**

*"It is a good thing for a boy to have captained his school or college eleven, but it is a very bad thing if, twenty years afterward, all that can be said of him is that he has continued to take an interest in football, baseball, or boxing, and has with him the memory that he was once captain."*

## Lesson 13
Offer All You Have **41**

*"I am as strong as a bull moose and you can use me to the limit."*

## Lesson 14
Self-Reliance: The Ultimate Test **42**

*"Excepting in a crowd I do not think a bodyguard is the least use. . . . [I]f there is any chance to break even with a would-be assassin I think the man himself, if alert and resolute, has a better opportunity to defend himself than any bodyguard would have to defend him."*

## Lesson 15
Work **44**

*"I have never won anything without hard labor and the exercise of my best judgment and careful planning and working long in advance."*

## Lesson 16
Try **45**

*"Life is a great adventure, and I want to say to you, accept it in such a spirit. I want to see you face it ready to do the best that lies in you to win out; and resolute,*

# 3 LEAD THE TEACHING LIFE

*the world in the shape in which we sent it, because none of the foreign countries of the greatest naval power believed that they themselves could do it; and they were proportionately impressed not only by the fact that we did it but by the way in which it was done—by the fact that the fleet, after being away for a year and a quarter, and circumnavigating the globe, came back, having kept to the minute every appointment on its schedule, and reached home in far better fighting trim as regards both men and ships than when it had sailed. That impressed all responsible statesmen abroad much more keenly even than it impressed our own people."*

## Lesson 43
### Avoid Sterile Debate **88**

*"I have not the slightest sympathy with debating contests in which each side is arbitrarily assigned a given proposition and told to maintain it without the least reference to whether those maintaining it believe in it or not. . . . What we need is to turn out of our colleges young men with ardent convictions on the side of right; not young men who can make good arguments for either right or wrong, as their interest bids them."*

## Lesson 44
### Avoid Fetish Thinking **89**

*"There is superstition in science quite as much as there is superstition in theology, and it is all the more dangerous because those suffering from it are profoundly convinced that they are freeing themselves from all superstition."*

## Lesson 45
### Study to Teach **90**

*"From the standpoint of the nation, and from the broader standpoint of mankind, scholarship is of worth chiefly when it is productive, when the scholar not merely receives or acquires, but gives."*

## Lesson 46
### Summon Them to a Higher Calling **91**

*"We, here in America, hold in our hands the hope of the world, the fate of the*

*coming years; and shame and disgrace will be ours if in our eyes the light of high resolve is dimmed, if we trail in the dust the golden hopes of men."*

*"History, taught for a directly and immediately useful purpose to pupils and the teachers of pupils, is one of the necessary features of a sound education in democratic citizenship."*

*"One of our defects as a nation is a tendency to use what have been called 'weasel words.' When a weasel sucks an egg the meat is sucked out of the egg; and if you use a 'weasel word' after another there is nothing left of the other."*

*"A stream cannot rise higher than its source."*

*"By his words and deeds he gave a defining and supporting frame for the aspirations of those insufficiently clear or strong to support their aspirations by their own endeavor. Men, in the hope of finding their better selves, attached themselves to him."*

**4 LEAD THE INNOVATIVE LIFE**

*"In advocating any measure we must consider not only its justice but its practicability."*

**Lesson 52**

Originate **102**

*"It is always better to be an original than an imitation."*

**Lesson 53**

Be an Innovative Organization Man **104**

*"The one thing abhorrent to the powers above the earth and under them is the hyphenated American—the "German-American," the "Irish-American," or the "native-American." Be Americans—pure and simple!"*

**Lesson 54**

Energize What's Right **105**

*"The corrupt men have been perfectly content to let their opponents monopolize all the virtue while they themselves have been permitted to monopolize all the efficiency."*

**Lesson 55**

Make Proactive Choices **106**

*"Any officer whose instinct was to stoke up before a crisis . . . could be trusted in wartime."*

**Lesson 56**

Don't Stand under a Corpse **107**

*Ansley Wilcox: "Don't you think it would be far better to do as the Cabinet has decided?"*

*Roosevelt: "No. It would be far worse."*

**Lesson 57**

To Think? To Act? To Innovate **109**

*"Mr. Roosevelt has taken the whole thing into his own hands, and is keeping it there in the quietest and most unobtrusive manner. He has done a very big and an entirely new thing."*

# 5 LEAD THE EXECUTIVE LIFE

**Lesson 79**

Fix Things, Not People **137**

*"War with the evil; but show no spirit of malignity toward the man who may be responsible for the evil. Put it out of his power to do wrong."*

**Lesson 80**

How Not to Sweat the Small Stuff **139**

*"It would be nonsense to refuse to allow a person to use the term 'Castile' unless the soap was made in Spain."*

**Lesson 81**

Create Excellence **140**

*"Success—the real success—does not depend upon the position you hold, but upon how you carry yourself in that position."*

**Lesson 82**

Give Everyone a Square Deal **141**

*"When I say I am for the square deal, I mean not merely that I stand for fair play under the present rules of the game, but that I stand for having those rules changed so as to work for a more substantial equality of opportunity and of reward for equally good service."*

**Lesson 83**

Practice the Art of the Fait Accompli **142**

*"I took the [Panama Canal Zone], started the canal, and then left Congress—not to debate the canal, but to debate me. But while the debate goes on the canal does too."*

**Lesson 84**

What to Do with Power **144**

*"The presidency should be a powerful office, and the President a powerful man, who will take every advantage of it . . ."*

[ 248 ]

**Lesson 85**

Fight Majority Misrule **145**

*"Whenever there is tyranny by the majority I shall certainly fight it."*

**Lesson 86**

How to Lead a Self-Governing Enterprise **146**

*"All of us, you and I, all of us together, want to rule ourselves, and we don't wish to have any body of outsiders rule us. That is what free government means."*

**Lesson 87**

Think Big Picture, Then Think Even Bigger **148**

*"I see no reason for believing that Russia is more advanced than Germany as regards international ethics, and Japan, with all her politeness and her veneer of western civilization, is at heart delighted to attack any and every western nation whenever the chances come and there is an opportunity for Japan to gain what she desires with reasonable safety. If Germany is smashed, it is perfectly possible that later she will have to be supported as a bulwark against [Russia] by the nations of Western Europe."*

**Lesson 88**

Speak the Language of Business **150**

*"No wise or generous soul will be content with a success which can be expressed only in dollars, but the soul which spurns all consideration of dollars usually drags down both itself and other souls into the gulf of pitiful failure."*

**Lesson 89**

Don't Be Too Smart **151**

*"I have only a second rate brain, but I think I have a capacity for action."*

**Lesson 90**

Don't Just Lead, Manage **152**

*"The bulk of government is not legislation but administration."*

*people up to it. This is always the attractive course; but in certain great crises it may be the wrong course."*

*sometimes they act very well, and sometimes they act very badly. We should consistently favor them when they act well, and as fearlessly oppose them when they act badly."*

**Lesson 114**

Know Your Decision Makers **191**

*"A vote is like a rifle: its usefulness depends upon the character of the user."*

**Lesson 115**

The Big Stick Revisited **192**

*"If a man continually blusters, if he lacks civility, a big stick will not save him from trouble; and neither will speaking softly avail, if back of the softness there does not lie strength, power."*

## 7 LEAD THE STEWARD'S LIFE

**Lesson 116**

The Essence of Stewardship **195**

*"It is not what we have that will make us a great nation; it is the way in which we use it."*

**Lesson 117**

Call on the Commonplace Virtues **196**

*"What is needed is common honesty, common sense, and common courage. We need the minor, the humdrum, the practical virtues—the commonplace virtues that are absolutely essential if we are ever to make this city what it should be. If these virtues are lacking, no amount of cleverness will answer."*

**Lesson 118**

Deem Denial Fatal **197**

*"A Nation should never fight unless forced to; but it should always be ready to fight."*

*team when you get to Harvard. But I think it a little silly to run any imminent risk of a serious smash simply to play on the second squad instead of the third."*

**Lesson 130**
Achieve Ethical Efficiency **213**
*"I have mighty little use for ethics that are applied with such inefficiency that no good results come."*

**Lesson 131**
Establish a Hierarchy of Rights **214**
*"The man who wrongly holds that every human right is secondary to his profit must now give way to the advocate of human welfare, who rightly maintains that every man holds his property subject to the general right of the community to regulate its use to whatever degree the public welfare may require it."*

**Lesson 132**
Character Is Destiny **215**
*"The United States of America has not the option as to whether it will or will not play a great part in the world. It must play a great part."*

**Lesson 133**
Regulate Power with Power **215**
*"It is essential that there should be organizations of labor. . . . Capital organizes and therefore labor must organize."*

**Lesson 134**
Make Every Deal a Square Deal **216**
*"We demand that big business give the people a square deal; in return we must insist that when anyone engaged in big business honestly endeavors to do right he shall himself be given a square deal."*

**Lesson 135**
Be Truly Conservative **218**
*"The only true conservative is the man who resolutely sets his face toward the future."*

# Index

# Sterling Books by
# Alan Axelrod